Sally Penni is a Barrister at Law with 21 years' experience. She is an advocate specialising in public law with an emphasis on vulnerability. She is an Approved Advocate trainer, a Bencher of the Honourable Society of Gray's Inn. She is a member of the Board of TAG – the Advocates Gateway.

A Practical Guide to Dealing with Vulnerable Witnesses in Criminal Courts and Beyond

A Practical Guide to Dealing with Vulnerable Witnesses in Criminal Courts and Beyond

Sally Penni
Barrister, Gray's Inn
LLB (Hons)

Law Brief Publishing

Published 2022 by Law Brief Publishing, an imprint of Law Brief Publishing Ltd
30 The Parks
Minehead
Somerset
TA24 8BT

www.lawbriefpublishing.com

Paperback: 978-1-913715-85-4

To my three children. For always being my motivation to keep practising law.

PREFACE

The 21 years of my career at the Bar have included conducting some high-profile cases in the youth court with young people to the crown court in a variety of courts and indeed with a number of vulnerable witnesses, complainants and victims as well as defendants and accused person. In each of those cases, I have been struck by the need to adapt to the witnesses needs and not the other way round.

The criminal courts in England and Wales have led the way in this. Especially in the use of intermediaries in the courts. Indeed I was one of the original trainers on the Intermediary course which was supported by the Ministry of justice and training provided by Professor Penny Cooper and David Wurtzel.

I now sit on the committee of Advocates Gateway (TAG).

In this book I look at some practical ways to keep abreast of vulnerable people in the court system. In criminal law and beyond.

It is not intended to be a bible on the subject but rather as a useful aid for Practitioners.

- WHO – who is vulnerable and what is vulnerability?
- WHAT – What laws and cases exist to help the vulnerable in court?
- HOW – How do you deal with them in Court
- WHERE – Where can advocates find support? Where can the vulnerable find assistance with their evidence?
- WHEN – When can you apply to use them?

What rules relate to their use in employment, civil law and family law cases? And outside of the UK.

I also look at how vulnerability is treated in other countries and beyond. Importantly what can we learn from looking at Monserrat, Chile, Australia, Tasmania just by way of example.

The consideration of other countries and jurisdictions will have to be the subject of another book.

I am especially interested in how the vulnerable are treated in the Coroner's Court for example.

I end this book with a reflection of practical things to think about.

Thank you for reading this book. I hope it helps whichever branch of the profession you are in.

The law described in this book is believed to be accurate and up-to-date as it was on 1st February 2022.

Sally Penni
Barrister at Law
Kenworthys Chambers, Manchester
4 Bream Buildings, London

ACKNOWLEDGEMENTS

This book has been a long time coming. I would like to thank the following.

Firstly, to my children for their patience.

Secondly, to Law Publishing for understanding that there was a need for this book.

Thirdly, Thank you to my clerks for their tolerance of me researching and writing this book.

Thank you to Kashmira Aukeer, a student for her assistance in some of the research for this book.

And finally thank you. Thank you for reading it. I hope it is useful in your practice whether as a trainee at the Bar or solicitor or a paralegal or CILEX or associate solicitor or junior or senior barrister or partner or even an expert. Thank you.

CONTENTS

CHAPTER ONE

WHO IS 'VULNERABLE'?

- Vulnerable is an *adjective* not a *noun* – so not 'the vulnerable' but situations in which a person may be 'vulnerable'
- No universal legal definition in England and Wales
- Criminal, family and civil law approach it differently
- Only legislation for criminal courts, though there are *practice directions* in many other courts and tribunals such as the family courts.

So it is important to remember to ask the following questions before the trial or hearing with the vulnerable person?

Often people use the following terminology to ask.

- Accommodations/adjustments/measures/special measures?
- Is ***a vulnerable accused person*** within the scope of these measures?
- Two words that people do seem to agree on: "**effective participation**"

  Can the person concerned have effective participation in the trial process without these adjustments?

  I would often ask myself this question. I would also ask whether we can achieve the best evidence rule.

Three proven Judicial Approaches.

Advocates should take these practical approaches.

1. Take a Witness specific approach
2. Make an Early applications for special measures
3. Hold a Ground Rules Hearings

Let us explore these in a little more detail.

Principle 1: Witness specific adjustments

Some examples:

- Supporter present
- Four-legged or even feathered friend

https://www.counselmagazine.co.uk/articles/therapy-animals-and-abe

- Cross-examination in the corridor
- Pre-recorded questioning
- Intermediary (communication support)

Principle 2: Early applications for measure/s

- The application should show clearly what is proposed and why (the application might be supported by a report from a teacher/doctor/ intermediary/speech therapist/carer etc)
- What are the wishes and feelings of the witness?
- *Ultimate issues: Are the proposed measures necessary to improve the quality of the witness's evidence?*
- *quality = completeness, coherence, accuracy

Principle 3: Ground rules hearings

- The application should show clearly what is proposed and why (the application might be supported by a report from a teacher/doctor/ intermediary/speech therapist/carer etc)

- What are the wishes and feelings of the witness?

- *Ultimate issues: Are the proposed measures necessary to improve the quality of the witness's evidence?*

- *quality = completeness, coherence, accuracy at least in my view anyway.

The Case Law

PS v PB **[2018] EWHC 1987 (Fam)**

> "Once it becomes clear to the court that it is required to hear a case "put" to a key factual witness where the allegations are serious and intimate and where the witnesses are themselves the accused and accuser, a "Ground Rules Hearing" (GRH) will always be necessary;"

GRH "in most cases, be conducted prior to the hearing of the factual dispute"

> "Judicial continuity between the GRH and the substantive hearing is to be regarded as essential

This case is a good summary for having ground rules hearing.

Case 2

R v Lubemba **(2014)**

- "[the judge is] duty bound to control the questioning of a witness. He is not obliged to allow a defence advocate to put their case. He is entitled to and should set reasonable time limits and to interrupt where he considers questioning is inappropriate."

- Must have GRH in all but "very exceptional circumstances"
- "an entirely reasonable step for a judge at the ground rules hearing to invite defence advocates to reduce their questions to writing in advance."

This was probably the pre cursor to written directions, written openings and much of advocacy now becoming written advocacy in the Crown court.

Now more than ever ones written work has become more crucial than ever. Therefore a practical advice is to advice that, If in doubt commit your arguments against a GRH or against a special measure in writing.

In summary, it was summarised beautifully in the case of

***Ajayi v Abu & Anor (labour exploitation : human trafficking : modern slavery) (Rev 1)* [2017] EWHC 1946 (QB)**

Where it was said:

> *"It is essential that the court fulfils its obligations in respect of proper measures to allow witnesses to give their testimony freely."*

The Advocates Tool Kit provides a very useful Kit for preparation in this area.

Indeed the advocates Training council encourages all advocates to read this.

Moreover, in the case of *R v Lubemba*

It was endorsed when it was said that,

> ***"The Toolkits may be downloaded at no cost from the Advocates Gateway Website. They provide excellent practical guides and are***

> *to be commended. They have been endorsed by the Lord Chief Justice in the Criminal Practice Directions Amendment No2 as best practice."*

Effect so far and the future.

It has been a Culture change for many advocates.

It has undoubtedly taken time. The early Resistance has largely gone and the feeling by defendants that they are prevented from having a fair trial by their defence advocates still remains.

There is a feeling sometimes that the introduction of special measures and video recordings have meant juries feel disconnected from complainants. As we have discovered during Covid-19 hearings and remote working, most things are better on a face-to-face basis.

1. And so Hesitation

2. Objections

3. Avoidance

Remain. Some colleagues have decided not to conduct certain cases on the bases that it takes away from the adversarial system and you can't teach old dogs new tricks.

In my view you can. This is a short-sighted approach and now with those practicing in the Youth Court now requiring to go on a special training, the ability to deal with vulnerable witnesses is crucial.

In my research for this book, I came across an interesting quote from Detective Chief Inspector Peter Yeomans, APM Child Abuse & Sex Crimes Squad, State Crime Command of NSW Police Force in Australia. He said that historically police have been the sole experts in obtaining evidence from child victims and was therefore hesitant in utilising someone external to this process. However he found that the use of Witness Intermediaries (working independently but alongside police) had been a 'watershed moment' in continually gaining the best evidence from child victims.

CHAPTER TWO

THE PRACTICAL APPROACH

Consider this approach

a. What is the legal basis for directing adjustments?

b. What is available in my jurisdiction or specialism?

c. Is there evidence that an adjustment is necessary for *this* witnesses? If not, obtain some evidence in a report, school report, psychologist, intermediaries.

d. Party applies for adjustments or the court of own motion directs?

e. A ground rules hearing is held. Make a note of issues to be dealt with at this hearing. For example use of dolls for body parts if a sexual assault case pr maps?

f. Reflect, learn

g. The appropriate reasonable adjustments which may be necessary for a litigant with a learning disability, including questioning techniques; some consideration of the advocates' gateway tool kit will often be useful here.

Remember the guidance in the Equal Treatment Bench Book, updated February 2021.

A good practical reminder for:

Good communication

> "8. Effective communication underlies the entire legal process: ensuring that everyone involved understands and is understood. Otherwise the legal process will be impeded or derailed.

9. This is a particular challenge in the context of remote hearings and judges will need to be sensitive to the many barriers that can reduce effective engagement in a hearing.

10. Understanding means understanding the evidence, the materials, the process, the meaning of questions and the answers to them.

11. If someone remains silent it does not necessarily mean that they understand. It may equally well mean that they do not understand, that they are unable to understand, that they feel intimidated or inadequate, that they are too inarticulate to speak up, or that they are otherwise unable to communicate properly.

12. It may be possible for a judge to test understanding by asking a supplementary question or summarising what he or she understands the position to be and asking if the party or witness agrees. It is usually most reliable to ask the party or witness to repeat back their understanding of what has been said to them.

13. Litigants in person may not have the courage to test the understanding of others or to admit that they do not fully understand a point.

14. People perceive the words and behaviour of others in terms of the cultural conventions with which they are most familiar. Our outlook is based on our own knowledge and experience, and this may lead to misinterpretation or a failure to understand those who are different or have different perspectives from us.

15. Effective communication requires an awareness of 'where a person is coming from' in terms of background, culture and special needs, and of the potential impact of those factors on the person's participation in the proceedings. It applies to witnesses, advocates, members of the court or tribunal staff and even members of the public who intervene when they should not.

16. Judges should try to put themselves in the position of those appearing before them. An appearance before a court or tribunal is a daunting and unnerving experience. As a result parties and witnesses may appear belligerent, hostile, rude, confused or emotional. A possible consequence is that they may not give a good account of themselves. The court or tribunal should endeavour to put them at their ease to enable them to do so. The more information and advice that is available before the hearing, the easier this will be to achieve.

17. Empathy is critical. As Judge Brian Doyle has said, 'Empathy is a quality all judges need – it is not partisanship, but understanding how someone is reacting in a process which is alien to most people'.

– Judge Brian Doyle, then President of the Employment Tribunals in England and Wales, on BBC Radio 4's Law in Action, March 2020."

Demonstrating fairness

Demonstrating fairness:

> "23. Fair treatment does not mean treating everyone in the same way: it means treating people equally in comparable situations. For example, a litigant in person with little understanding of law and procedure is not in a comparable situation to a QC. It is substantive equality that counts.
>
> 24. When parties do not get the outcome they would like or expect, it is particularly important that they feel they were fairly treated, fully heard and fully understood.
>
> 25. People who have difficulty coping with the language or procedures of the court or tribunal, and are perhaps less engaging litigants as a result, are entitled to justice in the same way as those who know how to use the legal system to their advantage. Any

disadvantage that a person faces in society should not be reinforced by the legal system.

26. Judges should identify a situation in which a person may be at a disadvantage owing to some personal attribute of no direct relevance to the proceedings, and take steps to remedy the disadvantage without prejudicing another party.

27. The sooner the disadvantage is identified, the easier it is to remedy it. Where possible, judges should ensure that information is obtained in advance of a hearing about any disability or medical or other circumstance affecting a person so that individual needs can be accommodated, eg access to interpreters, signers, large print, audiotape, oath-taking in accordance with different belief systems (including non-religious systems), more frequent breaks and special measures for vulnerable parties and witnesses can and should be considered. Very often the steps that will be required will be obvious and may require little more than pragmatic alterations to normal procedures.

28. Litigants in person should not be seen as an unwelcome problem for the court or tribunal. Judges may not be able to assist them with their case but can ensure they have every reasonable opportunity to present it."

CHAPTER THREE

CHILDREN, YOUNG PEOPLE AND VULNERABLE ADULTS

Who is vulnerable?

Witnesses and parties may be 'vulnerable' in court as a result of various factors, and reasonable adjustments need to be made. Although touching on the wider powers to make adjustments, a lot of this chapter focuses on the statutory regime in criminal cases for taking 'special measures' for 'vulnerable' witnesses. Those are defined as witnesses who are under 18, have a disability, or where various other factors apply. Family courts have increasingly adopted the regime of 'special measures' by way of 'participation directions', and certain other courts and tribunals have derived ideas and guidance to adopt within their own general procedures. Where reasonable adjustments for disabled people are required, the starting point would be:

(Physical Disability), then (Mental Disability this may include depression in which case simply things like sitting times and afternoon hearings are better listing.

If criminal proceedings are involved, this chapter would also be important.

Mental Capacity is addressed later on.

Is there a right for young and vulnerable witnesses to effective participation?

Accommodating a vulnerable person's needs (as required by case law, the **Equality Act 2010, the European Convention on Human Rights, the UN Convention on the Rights of the Child, the UN Convention on the Rights of Persons with Disabilities**) requires the court or tribunal to adopt a flexible approach in order to deal with cases justly.

Child witnesses and defendants have been shown to experience much higher levels of communication difficulty in the justice system than was previously recognised. This is also likely to be the case for vulnerable adult witnesses and the elderly. There also is a strong case for a distinct approach to the treatment of young adults in the criminal justice system. **The House of Commons Justice Committee** in its report, stated the following

> "The treatment of young adults in the criminal justice system', says that dealing effectively with young adults while the brain is still developing is crucial for them in making successful transitions to a crime-free adulthood. Children and vulnerable adults under stress can function at a lower level, making it harder for them to remember accurately and think clearly, and affecting their mental health."

CHAPTER FOUR

NEURODIVERSITY IN COURT

A growing number of witnesses are not neuro typical but are neuro diverse.

As mental health increases and we try and we try and be inclusive of neuro divergent people, it helps and assists to look at the range of conditions before making an application for special measures.

The important thing here is to have a report from an expert to back the condition.

What is neurodiversity?

Neurodiversity is an umbrella term covering a number of neurodevelopmental conditions.

These are:

- ADHD
- Autism
- Dyslexia
- Dyspraxia
- Dyscalculia
- Dysgraphia
- Tourette Syndrome

All of these conditions are neurodevelopmental, which means individuals are born with them and they don't go away – although neurodiverse people may well get better at coping with their condition(s). That's a key difference between a neurodiverse condition and a mental health issue – mental illnesses can fluctuate a great deal and it is possible to recover from them. But neurodiverse differences are lifelong.

There are no reliable statistics on how many people have a neurodiverse condition, but most people will have several neurodiverse people in their workplace, social circle and family. Diagnosis rates vary between countries, as do diagnostic criteria. Women and girls are much less likely to be diagnosed, particularly with autism and ADHD. Race can play a part too, with black people less likely to get an accurate diagnosis. Some people don't find out until quite late in life that they have a neurodiverse condition, and some never discover it at all.

Is neurodiversity a disability?

People with neurodiverse conditions are usually classified as disabled, and they do fall under the legal definition of disability as defined in the Equality Act. Neurodivergents (people with neurodiverse conditions) are also categorised as having special needs, learning difficulties or disorders. Some individuals identify with these labels and others do not. Many subscribe to the social model of disability. All neurodiverse people have individual needs and most will require reasonable adjustments at work.

Additional conditions

It's possible to have more than one neurodiverse diagnosis, and it's also possible to have additional conditions, such as learning difficulties or a physical disability. All neurodivergents have challenges with executive dysfunction, which means they have trouble doing tasks, activities or projects which most neurotypical (normal) people would not find challenging.

Common characteristics

The following characteristics are very common in neurodiverse individuals, regardless of what specific condition they have.

- Sensitive
- Empathetic
- Honest
- Creative
- Innovative
- Good at solving problems
- Mental health issues
- Difficult early experiences
- Difficulty fitting in
- At risk of manipulation
- People-pleasing
- Masking (concealing neurodiverse traits in order to fit in)
- Differences in processing/understanding information

Variations within neurodiversity

Every neurodiverse individual is different, and the conditions can vary a lot from person to person. While the conditions are present all the time, the symptoms can vary depending on support, coping strategies, other factors (such as stress or life changes) and so on. A person with a neurodiverse condition will always have the defining characteristic of that condition, but other characteristics may be stronger or weaker. Some neurodiverse people won't disclose their conditions and others may be unaware that they have a condition – this tends to be more common the older the person is.

Neurodiversity and mental health

Everyone's neurotype (the presence or absence of neurodiverse conditions) will be influenced by other experiences; for example, one's upbringing, family background, how one was taught and treated at school, social experiences and so on.

About half of people with dyslexia, ADHD or autism have depression and/or anxiety. Negative experiences because of the conditions are almost universal, so almost all neurodiverse people will be carrying emotional "baggage", even if they don't have a defined mental illness.

Many neurodiverse people who have not disclosed their condition (or don't know they have one) will take steps to avoid situations where their condition may be apparent. This could involve avoiding specific tasks, masking (trying to copy others to fit in), attempting to cope, taking longer over tasks, and anxiety. This can be very stressful which can then worsen symptoms and/or mental health conditions.

Dyslexia

Dyslexia is a specific learning disability. This means if you are dyslexic, you will experience problems in your ability to learn – mainly in reading and writing. Dyslexia has no effect on intelligence.

There are 3 main types of dyslexia:

- **Phonological (difficulty breaking sounds into parts)**
- **Surface (difficulty seeing entire words)**
- **Visual (visual processing and remembering words)**

Main characteristics of dyslexics:

- Visual
- Great spatial perception
- Challenges with reading and writing
- Difficulty with verbal communication
- Sees big picture rather than details
- Trouble with sequences
- Good at problem-solving
- Good pattern-recognition

Autism

Autism is also known as autistic spectrum disorder and autism spectrum disorder. One form of autism is known as Asperger's syndrome but this term is falling out of use. People with autism can be mildly or severely affected by the disorder and this can be referred to as high-functioning or low-functioning autism. Many autistic people and advocates reject functioning labels.

Autism pioneer Temple Grandin has proposed that there are 3 different types of autistics:

- Visual thinkers
- Verbal/logic thinkers
- Musical/mathematical thinkers

Main characteristics of autistics:

- Sensitive
- Organised/logical
- Factual
- Difficulty understanding neurotypicals
- Communication difficulties
- Clear
- Rigid
- Hyper-empathetic
- Non-judgemental
- Difficulty changing focus
- Routine-driven

ADHD

ADHD stands for Attention Deficit Hyperactivity Disorder. It's also called ADD – Attention Deficit Disorder – but this term is no longer widely used.

There are 3 types of ADHD:

- Hyperactive (always moving around)
- Inattentive (daydreaming)
- Mixed (both presentations)

Main characteristics of people with ADHD:

- Good under pressure
- Fidgety
- Daydreaming
- Rapid speech
- Quick-thinking
- Easily distracted
- Can multitask
- Can hyperfocus
- Time blindness
- Difficulty completing projects

Dyspraxia

Dyspraxia is also known as developmental co-ordination disorder. There are different kinds of dyspraxia but little consensus on what these are. Some types are described as:

- Verbal (difficulty producing clear speech)
- Oral (other difficulties with the mouth, such as eating)
- Motor (can affect fine and/or gross motor movement)
- Idea or Ideational (difficulties with co-ordination and sequences)
- Constructional/spatial (spatial awareness challenges)

Main characteristics of dyspraxics:

- Creative
- Original thinking
- Difficulties with fine motor movements
- Clumsy
- Good with strategic problem-solving
- Poor spatial awareness
- Caring
- Trouble with sequences
- Determined
- Hard-working
- Poor co-ordination

Dyscalculia

Dyscalculia is sometimes known as "maths dyslexia." As with other neurodivergent conditions, intelligence is unaffected.

Main characteristics of people with dyscalculia:

- Difficulty with maths
- Intuitive
- Poor sense of number and estimation

- Difficulty remembering basic facts
- Strategic problem-solvers
- Trouble with money
- Artistic/linguistic creativity
- Poor understanding of time
- Practical

Dysgraphia

Dysgraphia is a specific learning difficulty characterised by challenges with written information. This can be in the form of:

- Writing
- Spelling
- Typing

Main characteristics of people with dysgraphia include:

- Messy handwriting
- Difficulty with spelling
- Good conversationalists
- Unusual writing technique
- Creative
- Problem-solvers

- Good memories

Tourette Syndrome

Tourette Syndrome is also known as Tourette's Syndrome, Tourette's or TS. It is a neurological condition characterised by involuntary tics. Not all definitions of neurodiversity include Tourette's.

Main characteristics of people with Tourette's include:

- Physical tics (repetitive, involuntary movements)
- Vocal tics (involuntary making of sounds)
- Premonitory sensations (a sense that a tic will occur)
- Empathetic
- Echolalia (repeating words)
- Touching people or objects
- Good sense of humour
- Good cognitive control
- Energetic
- Verbal strengths

CHAPTER FIVE

VULNERABLE WITNESSES IN CRIMINAL PROCEEDINGS

Vulnerable witnesses, first recognised in the Youth Justice and Criminal Evidence Act 1999[1] would change the course of how witnesses were dealt with in the courts of England and Wales. The Act has 'radically altered the orthodox adversarial model for the reception of evidence from all witnesses under 17, and also from adult witnesses where the quality of their testimony is likely to be affected due to intimidation or due to their vulnerability because of the sexual nature of the offence charged or their mental or physical incapacity'.[2]

The full list of statutory special measures includes:

- Screening witness from accused under Section 23[3]
- Live TV link under Section 24[4]
- Exclusion of members of the public from the courtroom under Section 25[5]

---

[1] Youth Justice and Criminal Evidence Act 1999.

[2] Laura Hoyano, 'Striking a balance between the rights of defendants and vulnerable witnesses: will special measures directions contravene guarantees of a fair trial?' (2001) Crim LR 948.

[3] Youth Justice and Criminal Evidence Act 1999, s23.

[4] Youth Justice and Criminal Evidence Act 1999, s24.

[5] Youth Justice and Criminal Evidence Act 1999, s25.

- Removal of the judge's and barrister's wig and gowns under Section 26[6]

- Pre-recorded evidence-in-chief under Section 27[7]

- Pre-recorded cross-examination under Section 28[8]

- Questioning through an intermediary under Section 29[9]

- Artificial communication aids, such as a sign-board or voice synthesiser under Section 30.[10]

The court has to determine the eligibility of a witness needing special measures, by identifying them as vulnerable[11] or intimidated.[12] A special measures direction regarding the specified measures will be made under Section 19.[13] Under Section 19(2)[14] the court will distinguish the measures most appropriate to improve the quality of a witness's evidence.[15]

The court has the responsibility to consider all circumstances of the case, including witness opinions and if measures have the propensity to hinder evidence at trial. Henderson described the process of identifying

---

[6] Youth Justice and Criminal Evidence Act 1999, s26.

[7] Youth Justice and Criminal Evidence Act 1999, s27.

[8] Youth Justice and Criminal Evidence Act 1999, s28.

[9] Youth Justice and Criminal Evidence Act 1999, s29.

[10] Youth Justice and Criminal Evidence Act 1999, s30.

[11] Youth Justice and Criminal Evidence Act 1999, s16.

[12] Youth Justice and Criminal Evidence Act 1999, s17.

[13] Youth Justice and Criminal Evidence Act 1999, s19.

[14] Youth Justice and Criminal Evidence Act 1999, s19(2).

[15] ibid.

vulnerable witnesses, 'the most despised and vilified practice within the criminal trial'.[16]

The police play a significant role in the early identification of vulnerable witnesses, as they interview prosecution witnesses first.[17] The police have the difficult task of placing the witnesses into the categories of vulnerable or intimidated witnesses.[18] For their research, for the 1993 Royal Commission on Criminal Justice, Gudjonsson, Clare, Rutter and Pearse used screening interviews to estimate the proportion of vulnerable suspects.[19] They discovered, police identified four per cent of vulnerable witnesses, in comparison to their estimate of 15 – 20 per cent.[20] The Home Secretary in 1997, Jack Straw, announced the establishment of an Interdepartmental Working Group to undertake a wide-ranging review on the subject of vulnerable and intimidated witnesses.[21] The Government in June 1998 published *'Speaking up for Justice'* a report highlighting 78 recommendations on the treatment of vulnerable and intimidated witnesses in the Criminal Justice System.[22]

---

[16] Emily Henderson, 'All the proper protections – the Court of Appeal rewrites the rules for the cross-examination of vulnerable witness' (2014) 2 Crim LR 93.

[17] Mandy Burton, Roger Evans and Andrew Sanders, 'Implementing special measures for vulnerable and intimidated witnesses: the problem of identification' (2006) Crim LR 229, 232.

[18] ibid.

[19] Gisli Gudjonsson and others, *Persons at Risk during Interviews in Police Custody: The Identification of Vulnerabilities Royal Commission on Criminal Justice Research Study No 12* (HMSO, London 1993).

[20] ibid.

[21] Jenny McEwan, 'In defence of vulnerable witnesses: The Youth Justice and Criminal Evidence Act 1999' (2000) 4(1) 1.

[22] Home Office, *Speaking up for Justice: Report of the Interdepartmental Working Group on the Treatment of Vulnerable or Intimidated Witnesses in the Criminal Justice System* (Home Office 1998).

The opponents of the special measures directions proposals in Parliament were concerned they would breach Article 6(1) of the European Convention on Human Rights,[23] the right to a fair trial.[24] The Common Law adversarial trial model, unlike the system familiar to judges on the European Court of Human Rights, places primacy on the rights of the defendant.[25] This indicated the incompatibility with the model to balance the rights of the defendant(s) and witnesses.[26] Article 6(3)(d) of the European Court of Human Rights states 'to examine or have examined witnesses against him and to obtain the attendance and examination of witnesses on his behalf under the same conditions as witnesses against him'.[27] In *Doorson v Netherlands*,[28] the court accepted the witnesses' interests are protected by the European Convention on Human Rights and are a legitimate consideration in the fair trial proceedings.[29] In the same case, involving anonymous witnesses, the court accepted Article 6(3)(d)[30] guaranteed the right to examine witnesses; the circumstances whereby examination is conducted is a matter for the national courts to regulate.[31]

Screens

Screens are permitted under 'Section 23 of the Youth Justice and Criminal Evidence Act 1999:

---

23 Convention for the Protection of Human Rights and Fundamental Freedoms (European Convention on Human Rights, as amended) (ECHR) art 6(1).

24 Hoyano (n 2) 949.

25 ibid.

26 ibid.

27 Convention for the Protection of Human Rights and Fundamental Freedoms (European Convention on Human Rights, as amended) (ECHR) art 6(3)(d).

28 *Doorson v Netherlands* (1996) 22 EHRR 330.

29 Hoyano (n 2) 954.

30 Convention for the Protection of Human Rights and Fundamental Freedoms (European Convention on Human Rights, as amended) (ECHR) art 6(3)(d).

31 Hoyano (n 2) 955.

(1) A special measures direction may provide for the witness, while giving testimony or being sworn in court, to be prevented by means of a screen or other arrangement from seeing the accused.

(2) But the screen or other arrangement must not prevent the witness from being able to see, and to be seen by—

(a) the judge or justices (or both) and the jury (if there is one);

(b) legal representatives acting in the proceedings; and

(c) any interpreter or other person appointed (in pursuance of the direction or otherwise) to assist the witness.

(3) Where two or more legal representatives are acting for a party to the proceedings, subsection (2)(b) is to be regarded as satisfied in relation to those representatives if the witness is able at all material times to see and be seen by at least one of them'.[32]

A court considering whether to utilise a screen is directed by Section 19(2)(b).[33] Screens are available to adult and child witnesses, to protect them from being seen by the defendant when in the courtroom.[34] Courts can have permanent screens protecting the witness from seeing the defendant entering and exiting the courtroom.[35] Some courts have temporary screening arrangements and do not protect the witness from the defendant's sight.[36] The defendant may be removed from the dock when the witness enters and leaves the courtroom.[37] Screens prove to be

[32] Youth Justice and Criminal Evidence Act 1999, s23.

[33] Youth Justice and Criminal Evidence Act 1999, s19(2)(b).

[34] Mandy Burton, Roger Evans and Andrew Sanders, *'Are special measures for vulnerable and intimidated witnesses working? Evidence from the criminal justice agencies'* (United Kingdom Home Office 2006) 57.

[35] ibid.

[36] ibid.

[37] ibid.

the most effective in rape cases to shield the witness from the view of the defendant.[38]

The courts had discretion before the 1999 Act[39] to have screens placed around the witness box to prevent them from being able to see the defendant.[40]

The vulnerable witnesses who did not have an opportunity to use either live TV links or screens were asked if they would find screens helpful.[41] There were high levels of support for this special measure, with 60 per cent saying it would be advantageous.[42] 70 per cent of women agreed, in comparison with 46 per cent of men.[43] Also, 71 per cent of those experiencing intimidation admitted the screens would be beneficial.[44] The difficulty arises when a defendant representing himself wants to cross-examine a witness, in person, protected by a screen.

Evidence by live link

Under 'Section 24 of the Youth Justice and Criminal Evidence Act:

(1) A special measures direction may provide for the witness to give evidence by means of a live link.

---

[38] ibid.

[39] Youth Justice and Criminal Evidence Act 1999.

[40] Becky Hamlyn and others, '*Are special measures working? Evidence from Surveys of Vulnerable and Intimidated Witnesses*' (Home Office Research Study 2004) 71.

[41] ibid.

[42] ibid.

[43] ibid.

[44] ibid.

(1A) Such a direction may also provide for a specified person to accompany the witness while the witness is giving evidence by live link.

(1B) In determining who may accompany the witness, the court must have regard to the wishes of the witness.

(2) Where a direction provides for the witness to give evidence by means of a live link, the witness may not give evidence in any other way without the permission of the court.

(3) The court may give permission for the purposes of subsection (2) if it appears to the court to be in the interests of justice to do so, and may do so either—

(1) on an application by a party to the proceedings, if there has been a material change of circumstances since the relevant time, or

(2) of its own motion.

(4) In subsection (3) "the relevant time" means—

(a) the time when the direction was given, or

(b) if a previous application has been made under that subsection, the time when the application (or last application) was made'.[45]

The live link provision allows evidence to be obtained from a witness outside the courtroom whilst being seen and heard by the judge, jury and legal representatives.[46] It was for children to give evidence, in response to any difficulties encountered when at trial.[47] In *R (on the application of D)*

[45] Youth Justice and Criminal Evidence Act 1999, s24.

[46] Samantha Fairclough, 'It Doesn't Happen and I've Never Thought It Was Necessary for It to Happen: Barriers to Vulnerable Defendants Giving Evidence by Live Link in Crown Court Trials' (2017) 21 Int'l J Evidence & Proof 209, 210.

[47] ibid.

v Camberwell Green Youth Court[48] Baroness Hale, in paragraph 35, suggested Section 24(3),[49] permitting live link in the interests of justice, may be invoked where the child is anxious about giving evidence in the courtroom, is an escape route used by prosecutors where complainants wish to confront the defendant or see the jury.[50] Some courts, under Section 21(4)(b)[51] and Section 27(2)[52] exclude the use of live link, in the interests of justice, where a child wants to tell their story in the courtroom.

Adult witnesses, whose quality of evidence may be tarnished by their vulnerability, fear, or distress, can testify by using live link.[53] The main requirement the court must consider is whether the witness's quality of evidence will be improved.[54] Where proceedings take place before a Magistrates' court, but no suitable facilities are available, the court can sit at another Court where facilities are available.[55] An important factor to exemplify is the Act does not define whom a 'specified person to accompany the witness' can constitute to. In *Speaking Up for Justice*,[56] the Interdepartmental Working Group stated a vulnerable and intimidated witness should have a supporter with them, whom they are familiar with. Often, court ushers will be the ones to accompany vulnerable and intimidated witnesses into the room. For adult witnesses to give evidence by live link, they must suffer from a mental disorder,

---

[48] *R (on the application of D) v Camberwell Green Youth Court* [2005] UKHL 4.

[49] Youth Justice and Criminal Evidence Act 1999, s24(3).

[50] Laura Hoyano, 'Youth Justice and Criminal Evidence Act 1999: special measures directions – compliance with Article 6' (2005) 69(6) J Crim L 488, 491.

[51] Youth Justice and Criminal Evidence Act 1999, s21(4)(b).

[52] Youth Justice and Criminal Evidence Act 1999, s27(2).

[53] Fairclough (n 46) 210.

[54] McEwan (n 21) 6.

[55] ibid.

[56] Home Office, *Speaking up for Justice: Report of the Interdepartmental Working Group on the Treatment of Vulnerable or Intimidated Witnesses in the Criminal Justice System* (Home Office 1998).

under the Mental Health Act 1983[57] or significant impairment of intelligence or social function, as per the Youth Justice and Criminal Evidence Act 1999, Section 33A(5)(a).[58] Their ability to participate as a witness must be diminished under Section 33A(5)(b).[59] The purpose of the live link, per Section 33A(5)(c)[60] is to enable effective participation.

The live link provision also includes defence witnesses. Vulnerable defendant witnesses were excluded from the 1999 Act's scope until the addition of Section 33A[61] in 2006.[62] In *SC v UK*,[63] an 11-year-old defendant, ruled by the European Court of Human Rights, could not successfully participate in the trial, whilst having limited intellectual ability. Following the decision, the live link provision for defendant witnesses was incorporated into the Youth Justice and Criminal Act 1999[64].[65] Section 33A(4)(a) of the Youth Justice and Criminal Act 1999[66] states, for a child defendant to participate effectively as a witness, there must be a compromised level of intellectual ability or social functioning. The live link must improve their participation under Section 33A(4)(b).[67]

---

57 Mental Health Act 1983.

58 Youth Justice and Criminal Evidence Act 1999, s33A(5)(a).

59 Youth Justice and Criminal Evidence Act 1999, s33A(5)(b).

60 Youth Justice and Criminal Evidence Act 1999, s33(5)(c).

61 Youth Justice and Criminal Evidence Act 1999, s33A.

62 Fairclough (n 46) 210.

63 Case 60958/00 *SC v The United Kingdom* (2005) 40 EHRR 10.

64 Youth Justice and Criminal Evidence Act 1999.

65 Fairclough (n 46) 211.

66 Youth Justice and Criminal Evidence Act 1999, 33A(4)(a).

67 Youth Justice and Criminal Evidence Act 1999, 33A(4)(b).

Exclusion of members of the public from the courtroom

Evidence can be given in private per 'Section 25 of the Youth Justice and Criminal Act 1999:

(1) A special measures direction may provide for the exclusion from the court, during the giving of the witness's evidence, of persons of any description specified in the direction.

(2) The persons who may be so excluded do not include—

(a) the accused,

(b) legal representatives acting in the proceedings, or

(c) any interpreter or other person appointed (in pursuance of the direction or otherwise) to assist the witness.

(3) A special measures direction providing for representatives of news gathering or reporting organisations to be so excluded shall be expressed not to apply to one named person who—

(a) is a representative of such an organisation, and

(b) has been nominated for the purpose by one or more such organisations, unless it appears to the court that no such nomination has been made.

(4) A special measures direction may only provide for the exclusion of persons under this section where—

(a) the proceedings relate to a sexual offence or an offence under section 1 or 2 of the Modern Slavery Act 2015; or

(b) it appears to the court that there are reasonable grounds for believing that any person other than the accused has sought, or will seek, to intimidate the witness in connection with testifying in the proceedings.

(5) Any proceedings from which persons are excluded under this section (whether or not those persons include representatives of news gathering or reporting organisations) shall nevertheless be taken to be held in public for the purposes of any privilege or exemption from liability available in respect of fair, accurate and contemporaneous reports of legal proceedings held in public'.[68]

Prior to the 1999 Act,[69] courts in England and Wales had the discretion to clear the public gallery, although it was rarely used.[70] The Act now places the provision on a statutory footing for cases involving sexual offences or intimidation.[71] Section 46 of the Act[72] allows a nominee of the press to stay in court, to report the case.[73]

Removal of the judge's and barrister's wig and gowns

Section 26 of the Youth Justice and Criminal Evidence Act 1999 'provides for the wearing of wigs or gowns to be dispensed with during the giving of the witness's evidence'.[74] This measure is mostly associate with child witnesses, to help them give the best evidence.[75]

Video recorded interviews

Video recorded interviews have to be conducted per the *Memorandum of Good Practice*[76] by teams from child protection units.[77] These are often

[68] Youth Justice and Criminal Evidence Act 1999, s25.

[69] Youth Justice and Criminal Evidence Act 1999.

[70] Hamlyn (n 40) 72.

[71] ibid.

[72] Youth Justice and Criminal Evidence Act 1999, s46.

[73] Hamlyn (n 40) 72.

[74] Youth Justice and Criminal Evidence Act 1999, s25.

[75] Hamlyn (n 40) 73.

[76] Home Office Department of Health, *Memorandum of Good Practice on Videotaped Interviews with Child Witnesses in Criminal Proceedings* (Home Office 1992).

[77] McEwan (n 21) 6.

police officers and social workers with considerable experience in child abuse.[78] The court has the discretion to exclude a video recorded interview if the witness will not be available for cross-examination, in court or on videotape.[79] The court may also exclude a video recorded interview if there is insufficient information regarding the circumstance the recording was provided.[80]

In addition, a witness must attend court unless the parties agree cross-examination is unnecessary or the cross-examination takes place by videotaped evidence.[81] If an adult witness is using a video recorded interview on the grounds of fear, there is a probability the recording will take place shortly before the trial.[82]

The rationale of video recorded interviews is to reduce the stress on witnesses. However, some critics have highlighted the measures makes it easier for witnesses to lie.[83] Another rationale of video recorded interviews is a memory-refreshing document.[84] Previous consistent or inconsistent statements can be identified through the video. If a video recording exists but is not presented in the place of evidence-in-chief, at the trial, the witness may be cross-examined on discrepancies between what is said at trial and in the interview. A significant problem with video recording interviews is how the court's discretion to exclude evidence could have adverse effects on the fairness of proceedings,[85] under Section 78 of the Police and Criminal Evidence Act 1984.[86] In the case of *Parker*,[87] a child

---

[78] ibid.

[79] McEwan (n21) 7.

[80] ibid.

[81] ibid.

[82] ibid.

[83] ibid.

[84] McEwan (n21) 8.

[85] McEwan (n21) 9.

[86] Police and Criminal Evidence Act 1984.

[87] *R v Parker* [1996] Crim LR 511 CA.

withdrew an accusation recorded during a video interview.[88] Although the defence requested for the exclusion under Section 78,[89] the prosecution proceeding in playing the tape.[90] The defence's objection was upheld by the Court of Appeal on the grounds of unfairness.[91] The child should have been offered the opportunity to give evidence via live link.[92]

Plotnikoff and Woolfson conducted a study of 182 young witnesses, involved in legal proceedings.[93] They found most were anxious before trial; experiencing delays or rescheduling during the court process.[94] Half of them said they did not understand questions put to them whilst in court.[95] Additionally, they reported difficulties regarding the questioner's tone and approach; describing them as 'sarcastic', 'intimidating', 'relentless' and 'cross'.[96]

The provision states children who are alleged victims of or witnesses to sexual offences, are entitled to give their direct testimony by way of video recorded interview and to be cross-examined and re-examined in a videotaped pre-trial hearing.[97] Where a child will testify about violent offences, kidnapping or neglect, the cross-examination must be conducted at trial, through a live video link.[98] Other alternative options

---

88 McEwan (n21) 9.

89 Police and Criminal Evidence Act 1984.

90 McEwan (n21) 9.

91 ibid.

92 ibid.

93 Joyce Plotnikoff and Richard Woolfson, 'Measuring up? Evaluating implementation of government commitments to young witnesses in criminal proceedings' (NSPCC London 2009) 108.

94 ibid.

95 ibid.

96 ibid.

97 Hoyano (n 2) 948.

98 Hoyano (n 2) 949.

may be requested, whereby the court orders an optional pre-trial hearing or the court is satisfied the video link would not maximise the quality of evidence.[99]

Pre-recorded evidence-in-chief

Pre-recorded evidence-in-chief is stated in 'Section 27 of the Youth Justice and Criminal Evidence Act 1999:

(1) A special measures direction may provide for a video recording of an interview of the witness to be admitted as evidence in chief of the witness.

(2) A special measures direction may, however, not provide for a video recording, or a part of such a recording, to be admitted under this section if the court is of the opinion, having regard to all the circumstances of the case, that in the interests of justice the recording, or that part of it, should not be so admitted.

(3) In considering for the purposes of subsection (2) whether any part of a recording should not be admitted under this section, the court must consider whether any prejudice to the accused which might result from that part being so admitted is outweighed by the desirability of showing the whole, or substantially the whole, of the recorded interview.

(4) Where a special measures direction provides for a recording to be admitted under this section, the court may nevertheless subsequently direct that it is not to be so admitted if—

(a) it appears to the court that—

(i) the witness will not be available for cross-examination (whether conducted in the ordinary way or in accordance with any such direction), and

[99] ibid.

(ii) the parties to the proceedings have not agreed that there is no need for the witness to be so available; or

(3) any Criminal Procedure Rules requiring disclosure of the circumstances in which the recording was made have not been complied with to the satisfaction of the court.

(5) Where a recording is admitted under this section—

(a) the witness must be called by the party tendering it in evidence, unless—

(i) a special measures direction provides for the witness's evidence on cross-examination to be given in any recording admissible under section 28, or

(ii) the parties to the proceedings have agreed as mentioned in subsection (4)(a)(ii); and

(b) the witness may not without the permission of the court give evidence in chief otherwise than by means of the recording as to any matter which, in the opinion of the court, is dealt with in the witness's recorded testimony.

(6) Where in accordance with subsection (2) a special measures direction provides for part only of a recording to be admitted under this section, references in subsections (4) and (5) to the recording or to the witness's recorded testimony are references to the part of the recording or testimony which is to be so admitted.

(7) The court may give permission for the purposes of subsection (5)(b) if it appears to the court to be in the interests of justice to do so, and may do so either—

(a) on an application by a party to the proceedings, or

(b) of its own motion.

(8) ...

(9) The court may, in giving permission for the purposes of subsection (5)(b), direct that the evidence in question is to be given by the witness by means of a live link;

(9A) If the court directs under subsection (9) that evidence is to be given by live link, it may also make such provision in that direction as it could make under section 24(1A) in a special measures direction.

(10) A magistrates' court inquiring into an offence as examining justices under section 6 of the Magistrates' Courts Act 1980 may consider any video recording in relation to which it is proposed to apply for a special measures direction providing for it to be admitted at the trial in accordance with this section.

(11) Nothing in this section affects the admissibility of any video recording which would be admissible apart from this section'.[100]

Davies, Wilson, Mitchell and Milsom found there was strong support for video interviews amongst child protection workers.[101] Lawyers were hesitant in using video recorded evidence-in-chief to increase the accuracy of evidence.[102] Ellison (2001) suggested there are structural challenges with the quality of video interviews.[103] They are difficult to overcome, regardless of the guidance on how to conduct interviews. Burton, Evans and Sanders agree with Ellison stating 'an interview designed both to investigate and provide evidence of an offence will never

[100] Youth Justice and Criminal Evidence Act 1999.

[101] Graham Davies and others, *Videotaping children's evidence: An* evaluation (Home Office 1995).

[102] Mandy Burton, Roger Evans and Andrew Sanders, *'Are special measures for vulnerable and intimidated witnesses working? Evidence from the criminal justice agencies'* (United Kingdom Home Office 2006) 53.

[103] Louise Ellison, *The Adversarial Process and the Vulnerable Witness* (Oxford University Press 2001) 57.

be carried out in the same way a barrister at trial attempts to construct a credible narrative'.[104]

Burton emphasises a significant benefit of video interviews, as they enable 'evidence to be recorded in close proximity to the complaint, producing a more detailed and accurate account'.[105] This advantage can be tarnished by the delay in making the video after the criminal act has taken place. Another disadvantage is the witness goes into cross-examination unprepared. Ellison describes this as being 'plunged directly into hostile cross-examination at trial without the 'warm up' that examination in chief provides'.[106] The long delay between the pre-recorded evidence-in-chief and cross-examination has the potential to undermine the witness's credibility and exposing inconsistencies in their evidence.[107]

Witnesses are allowed to watch their pre-recorded examination-in-chief before the cross-examination. There have been occasions whereby child witnesses have been offered to watch their video recordings before the trial. This is not always offered because children can find it distressing to re-watch their video interview. Some judges in courts, stopped the video recording when they could see the witnesses becoming distressed.

Regarding the European Convention on Human Rights, Article 6(3)(d)[108] does not stipulate when or how a witness must be available for

[104] Mandy Burton, Roger Evans and Andrew Sanders, *'Are special measures for vulnerable and intimidated witnesses working? Evidence from the criminal justice agencies'* (United Kingdom Home Office 2006) 53.

[105] Mandy Burton, Roger Evans and Andrew Sanders, *'Are special measures for vulnerable and intimidated witnesses working? Evidence from the criminal justice agencies'* (United Kingdom Home Office 2006) 54.

[106] Louise Ellison, *The Adversarial Process and the Vulnerable Witness* (Oxford University Press 2001) 57.

[107] Mandy Burton, Roger Evans and Andrew Sanders, *'Are special measures for vulnerable and intimidated witnesses working? Evidence from the criminal justice agencies'* (United Kingdom Home Office 2006) 54.

[108] Convention for the Protection of Human Rights and Fundamental Freedoms (European Convention on Human Rights, as amended) (ECHR) art 6(3)(d).

examination.[109] In the *Redbridge Youth Court* case,[110] the Division Court held unanimously the admission of video interviews under the Criminal Justice Act 1988[111] does not offence Article 6.[112]

Pre-recorded cross-examination or re-examination

Pre-recorded cross-examination and re-examination both fall under the scope of 'Section 28 of the Youth Justice and Criminal Act 1999:

(1) Where a special measures direction provides for a video recording to be admitted under section 27 as evidence in chief of the witness, the direction may also provide—

(a) for any cross-examination of the witness, and any re-examination, to be recorded by means of a video recording; and

(b) for such a recording to be admitted, so far as it relates to any such cross-examination or re-examination, as evidence of the witness under cross-examination or on re-examination, as the case may be.

(2) Such a recording must be made in the presence of such persons as Criminal Procedure Rules or the direction may provide and in the absence of the accused, but in circumstances in which—

(a) the judge or justices (or both) and legal representatives acting in the proceedings are able to see and hear the examination of the witness and to communicate with the persons in whose presence the recording is being made, and

109 Hoyano (n 2) 957.

110 R (on the application of) DPP v Redbridge Youth Court [2001] EWHC Admin 209.

111 Criminal Justice Act 1988.

112 Convention for the Protection of Human Rights and Fundamental Freedoms (European Convention on Human Rights, as amended) (ECHR) art 6.

(b) the accused is able to see and hear any such examination and to communicate with any legal representative acting for him.

(3) Where two or more legal representatives are acting for a party to the proceedings, subsection (2)(a) and (b) are to be regarded as satisfied in relation to those representatives if at all material times they are satisfied in relation to at least one of them.

(4) Where a special measures direction provides for a recording to be admitted under this section, the court may nevertheless subsequently direct that it is not to be so admitted if any requirement of subsection (2) or Criminal Procedure Rules or the direction has not been complied with to the satisfaction of the court.

(5) Where in pursuance of subsection (1) a recording has been made of any examination of the witness, the witness may not be subsequently cross-examined or re-examined in respect of any evidence given by the witness in the proceedings (whether in any recording admissible under section 27 or this section or otherwise than in such a recording) unless the court gives a further special measures direction making such provision as is mentioned in subsection (1)(a) and (b) in relation to any subsequent cross-examination, and re-examination, of the witness.

(6) The court may only give such a further direction if it appears to the court—

(a) that the proposed cross-examination is sought by a party to the proceedings as a result of that party having become aware, since the time when the original recording was made in pursuance of subsection (1), of a matter which that party could not with reasonable diligence have ascertained by then, or

(b) that for any other reason it is in the interests of justice to give the further direction.

(7) Nothing in this section shall be read as applying in relation to any cross-examination of the witness by the accused in person (in a case where the accused is to be able to conduct any such cross-examination)'.[113]

There were objections against the proposal because if further cross-examination was needed after the creation of the recording, the child would be put through the process twice.[114] The Working Group offered a solution – preventing further cross-examination unless new material came to light.[115]

Section 28(1)[116] provides for the recording of cross-examination and evidence-in-chief, whereby both are video recorded interviews. The recording has to be created, abiding by court rules, direction provided or absence of the accused.[117] If the accused is present, they must see and hear the examination and communicate with their lawyer.[118] This special measure is not available where the cross-examination of the witness is to be conducted by the accused in person.[119]

Examination of witness through an intermediary

Examination of a witness using an intermediary is covered by 'Section 29 of the Youth Justice and Criminal Evidence Act 1999:

(1) A special measures direction may provide for any examination of the witness (however and wherever conducted) to be conducted

[113] Youth Justice and Criminal Evidence Act 1999, s28.

[114] McEwan (n 21) 9.

[115] ibid.

[116] Youth Justice and Criminal Evidence Act 1999, s28(1).

[117] ibid.

[118] ibid.

[119] ibid.

through an interpreter or other person approved by the court for the purposes of this section ("an intermediary").

(2) The function of an intermediary is to communicate—

(a) to the witness, questions put to the witness, and

(b) to any person asking such questions, the answers given by the witness in reply to them,

and to explain such questions or answers so far as necessary to enable them to be understood by the witness or person in question.

(3) Any examination of the witness in pursuance of subsection (1) must take place in the presence of such persons as Criminal Procedure Rules or the direction may provide, but in circumstances in which—

(a) the judge or justices (or both) and legal representatives acting in the proceedings are able to see and hear the examination of the witness and to communicate with the intermediary, and

(b) (except in the case of a video recorded examination) the jury (if there is one) are able to see and hear the examination of the witness.

(4) Where two or more legal representatives are acting for a party to the proceedings, subsection (3)(a) is to be regarded as satisfied in relation to those representatives if at all material times it is satisfied in relation to at least one of them.

(5) A person may not act as an intermediary in a particular case except after making a declaration, in such form as may be prescribed by Criminal Procedure Rules, that he will faithfully perform his function as intermediary.

(6) Subsection (1) does not apply to an interview of the witness which is recorded by means of a video recording with a view to its admission as evidence in chief of the witness; but a special measures direction may provide for such a recording to be admitted under section 27 if the interview was conducted through an intermediary and—

(a) that person complied with subsection (5) before the interview began, and

(b) the court's approval for the purposes of this section is given before the direction is given.

(7) Section 1 of the Perjury Act 1911 (perjury) shall apply in relation to a person acting as an intermediary as it applies in relation to a person lawfully sworn as an interpreter in a judicial proceeding; and for this purpose, where a person acts as an intermediary in any proceeding which is not a judicial proceeding for the purposes of that section, that proceeding shall be taken to be part of the judicial proceeding in which the witness's evidence is given'.[120]

Registered intermediaries have been facilitating communication with vulnerable witnesses since 2004.[121] The Witness Intermediary Scheme was first introduced as a pilot project.[122] Section 29 of the Youth Justice and Criminal Evidence Act 1999 defined intermediary as any person who is registered on the national database, the Intermediary Register.[123]

---

120 Youth Justice and Criminal Evidence Act 1999, s29.

121 McEwan (n 21) 7.

122 ibid.

123 Youth Justice and Criminal Evidence Act 1999, s28.

What is the 'Code of Practice for Registered Intermediaries? It sets out the duties and expectations of intermediaries below. They are:

1. The main responsibility of the intermediary is to enable complete, coherent and accurate communication to take place between a witness who requires special measures and the court.

2. Intermediaries must have a clear and comprehensive understanding of the responsibilities and duties of their role within the CJS, including their primary responsibility to the court.

3. They must conduct themselves in a professional and courteous manner at all times.

4. They must be familiar with and observe the terms and conditions and procedures that govern their assignment.

5. They should identify the sources of advice, information and materials required in order to ensure a clear understanding of the special needs of the witness.

6. They must carry out a functional assessment of the communication needs of the witness and make an informed professional judgement of the time required to enable them to carry out the assessment satisfactorily.

7. They will use the background information provided and will meet with the witness, his or her relatives, supporter, carer or relevant professionals to acquaint themselves fully with the knowledge and understanding required to carry out the assignment successfully.

8. They must not enter discussions, give advice or express opinions concerning the evidence the witness is to present or any aspect of the case that could contaminate the evidence or lead to an allegation of rehearsing or coaching the witness.

9. They must keep the co-ordinator and other appropriate parties informed of any difficulties that may arise in the course of the assignment that may affect the prospects of best evidence being given.

10. They must hold meetings with witnesses within a time-scale agreed with the co-ordinator and in appropriate venues.

11. They must make clear the purpose of the meetings and structure meetings in a way that allows sufficient time to assess the needs of the witness and to gain the confidence and trust of the witness.

12. They must record and communicate to the co-ordinator any dissatisfaction expressed by the witness with either the intermediary or the procedure being followed.

13. They must ensure the witness is satisfied with the outcome of the assessment and understands the role of the intermediary, particularly in the context of the court appearance.

14. They must conduct themselves in court in a manner that facilitates complete, coherent and accurate communication between the witness and the court.

15. They must not change the content of what is being said or attempt to improve or elaborate what has been said. Any actions that may improve understanding without changing meaning or the sense of what is being said, such as conveying the meaning of gestures the witness may make, must be taken only with the explicit understanding and consent of the court.

16. They must disclose to the court any difficulties encountered, such as limitations in their professional experience and training, and seek the court's guidance about action that may be taken that is consistent with best evidence.

17. They must intervene only to seek clarification from the court or to draw the court's attention to any difficulty the witness may be

experiencing in understanding what is being said or that may be distressing the witness.

18. They must respect at all times the authority and judgement of the court.

19. They must complete, at the conclusion of each assignment a monitoring and evaluation form that will contribute to efforts to improve the quality of the service.

20. They must recognise that an intermediary's duty to the court remains paramount. They must understand the different obligations regarding disclosure of information between the prosecution and the defence legal teams and must maintain their professional integrity in relation to these different obligations.

21. They must notify the Intermediaries Registration Board (IRB) immediately of any criminal investigation or proceedings against them or any other complaint or investigation into their conduct or competence.

22. They must notify the Intermediaries Registration Board of the result of any adverse criminal records disclosure check carried out on them. (i.e. any result where a conviction is recorded other than already disclosed to the IRB)'.[124]

A witness may be eligible for an intermediary, if:

- 'They are under the age of 18 at the time of the hearing; or

[124] Ministry of Justice 'Registered Intermediary Procedural Guidance' (September 2020) <https://assets.publishing.service.gov.uk/government/uploads/system/uploads/attachment_data/file/955316/registered-intermediary-procedural-guidance-manual.pdf> accessed 23 June 2021.

- If the court considers the quality of evidence given by the witness is likely to be diminished by:
- a) a mental disorder (under the Mental Health Act 1983); or
- b) a significant impairment of intelligence or social functioning; or
- c) a physical disability or physical disorder'.[125]

We must not fear them but welcome them in my view because as was expressed intermediaries are a remarkable and highly effective tool for improving the quality of communication in the courtroom; however, they are used in very few difficult cases.[126]

Aids to communication

Under Section 30, 'a special measures direction may provide for the witness, while giving evidence (whether by testimony in court or otherwise), to be provided with such device as the court considers appropriate with a view to enabling questions or answers to be communicated to or by the witness despite any disability or disorder or other impairment which the witness has or suffers from'.[127]

---

125 Youth Justice and Criminal Evidence Act 1999, s16.

126 Henderson (n 16) 94.

127 Youth Justice and Criminal Evidence Act 1999, s30.

CHAPTER SIX

VULNERABLE WITNESSES IN FAMILY COURTS PROCEEDINGS

Lord Wolfson of Tredegar QC, Parliamentary Under Secretary of State, Ministry of Justice stated "Some of the most vulnerable in our society come before the family courts, and we are absolutely determined that we offer them every protection. We will ensure that victims of domestic abuse are not intimidated by their abuser in court".[128]

Special measures in family proceedings are protected in Part 38 of the Family Procedure Rules 2010 and supported by Practice Direction 3AA.[129] These rules ensure victims of domestic abuse, other parties and witnesses are eligible for special measures if their quality of evidence is diminished by their vulnerability. Like in criminal proceedings, before determining what special measures are applicable, the court has to assess if a victim is 'vulnerable'.

The court must consider, under 'paragraph 3A.5 of the Family Procedure Rules 2017:

(1) whether the quality of evidence given by a party or witness is likely to be diminished by reason of vulnerability and, if so whether it is necessary to make one or more participation directions.

---

[128] Home Office, 'Policy Paper Special measures in family proceedings' (May 2021) <https://www.gov.uk/government/publications/domestic-abuse-bill-2020-factsheets/special-measures-in-family-proceedings#what-are-special-measures> accessed 23 June 2021.

[129] The Family Procedure (Amendment No.3) Rules 2017.

(2) Before making such participation directions, the court must consider any views expressed by the party or witness about giving evidence'.[130]

Under 'paragraph 3A.7 highlights what the courts must regards when making one or more directions:

(a) whether the party or witness—

(i) suffers from mental disorder or otherwise has a significant impairment of intelligence or social functioning;

(ii) has a physical disability or suffers from a physical disorder; or

(iii) is undergoing medical treatment;

(b) the nature and extent of the information before the court;

(c) the issues raised in the proceedings;

(d) whether a matter is contentious;

(e) the age, maturity and understanding of the party or witness;

(f) the social and cultural background and ethnic origins of the party or witness;

(g) the domestic circumstances and religious beliefs of the party or witness;

(h) any behaviour towards the party or witness on the part of—

(i) any other party to the proceedings or members of the family or associates of that other party;

[130] The Family Procedure (Amendment No.3) Rules 2017, para 3A.5.

(ii) any members of the family of the party or witness;

(i) any questions which the court is putting or causing to be put to a witness in accordance with section 31G(6) of the 1984 Act;

(j) any characteristic of the party or witness which is relevant to the participation directions which may be made;

(k) whether any measure is available to the court;

(l) the costs of any available measure; and

(m) any matters set out in Practice Direction 3AA'.[131]

The Family Procedure Rules were amended in November 2017, to implement provisions about vulnerable witnesses.[132] In a further attempt to reform family proceedings, in 2017 The Ministry of Justice amended the Prisons and Courts Bill to include statutory provisions. The amendment would prohibit cross-examination of vulnerable witnesses by alleged abusers in family courts to prevent a person with unspent convictions, charged with specified offences' from cross-examining the victim.[133] Due to the 2017 general election, the Bill did not go through.

In *Re A (A minor)*,[134] Justice Hayden outlined the cross-examination of vulnerable witnesses in family proceedings were a prevalent issue. During the case, special measures were in place. Justice Hayden made it evident, it was extremely disturbing to witness a woman be cross-examined by a perpetrator. In July 2020, the House of Commons passed the Domestic Abuse Bill, as promised by the current Conservative government. Once passed through the House of Lords, it is set to become law. The Bill includes provisions to protect vulnerable victims of domestic abuse.

---

131 The Family Procedure (Amendment No.3) Rules 2017, 3A.7.

132 The Family Procedure (Amendment No 3) Rules 2017.

133 Katherine Res Pritchard and Kate Williams, 'Cross-examination of vulnerable persons in family law proceedings' [2019] 49(1) Fam Law 48.

134 *Re A (A minor)* [2017] EWHC 1195 (Fam).

There will be an automatic ban on cross-examination in person where a party has been convicted, cautioned or charged with offences against the witness. The ban will also cover on-notice protective injunctions between the party and witness or where there is other evidence of abuse.

The Family Justice System is severely lagging behind its criminal counterpart in respect to special measures for protecting vulnerable witnesses.[135] Although safeguard measures are put in place for the protection of individuals during the family court proceedings, victims can still face cross-examination from alleged perpetrators of abuse.[136] I frequently check the drafted questions of colleagues in the family courts.

The Advocates Gateway

The Advocate's Gateway (TAG) is Extremely practical and helpful toolkits are available on its website at

www.theadvocatesgateway.org including:

1. Ground rules hearings and the fair treatment of vulnerable people in court.
2. Ground rules hearing checklist (although written with criminal proceedings in mind, may also be useful for other courts/tribunals where there is an application for the ground rules approach).
3. 1a. Case management in criminal cases when a witness or defendant is vulnerable. Essential questions checklist.
4. 8. Effective participation of young defendants.

---

[135] Katherine Res Pritchard and Kate Williams, 'Cross-examination of vulnerable persons in family law proceedings' [2019] 49(1) Fam Law 48.

[136] ibid.

5. Identifying vulnerability in witnesses and parties and making adjustments.

CHAPTER SEVEN

VULNERABLE WITNESSES IN EMPLOYMENT TRIBUNALS

April 2020 marked a significant change in employment tribunal proceedings with the introduction of a Presidential Guidance on vulnerable parties and witnesses. The purpose of the Presidential Guidance is to 'focus all the attention of all employment tribunal judges and members, parties, witnesses and representatives on the issue of vulnerability, however that issue might arise of appear'.[137]

To identify a vulnerable witness in employment proceedings, the Presidential Guidance says, 'A good test of vulnerability might be whether the person is likely to suffer fear or distress in giving evidence because of their own circumstances or those relating to the case'.[138] The Presidential Guidance highlights 'vulnerable parties and witnesses in Employment Tribunal proceedings are not a homogenous group'.[139] There are some factors such as mental and physical disability, intellectual and social disadvantages that can be barriers to access justice in employment litigation.[140]

Paragraph 14 of the Presidential Guidance outline 19 factors when making directions or order to facilitate participation:

---

[137] Employment Tribunal, 'Presidential Guidance: Vulnerable parties and witnesses in Employment Tribunal proceedings' (July 2021) < https://www.judiciary.uk/wp-content/uploads/2013/08/ET-Presidential-Guidance-on-Vulnerable-Parties-and-Witnesses-22-April-2020.pdf> accessed 9 July 2021, para 4.

[138] ibid.

[139] ibid, para 9.

[140] ibid, para 9.

1. The impact of any actual or perceived or potential intimidation of a party or witness.

2. Whether the party or witness has or may have a mental disability or other mental health condition.

3. Whether the party or witness otherwise has or may have a significant impairment of intelligence or social functioning.

4. Whether the party or witness has or may have a physical disability or other physical health condition.

5. Whether the party or witness is undergoing medical treatment.

6. The nature and extent of the information before the tribunal (including any medical or other evidence).

7. The issues arising in the proceedings.

8. Whether a matter is contentious.

9. The age, maturity and understanding of the party or witness.

10. The social and cultural background of the party or witness.

11. The ethnic origins of the party or witness (so far as might be relevant).

12. The domestic circumstances of the party or witness.

13. The religious beliefs of the party or witness (so far as might be relevant).

14. Any questions which the tribunal will put (or cause to be put) to a witness.

15. Any characteristic of the party or witness which is relevant to the direction or order that may be made.

16. Whether any measure is available to the tribunal.

17. The costs of any available measure.

18. The view of the vulnerable party or witness.

19. Any other relevant matter.[141]

When the issues arise, parties have to consider 'whether a party's application in the proceedings is likely to be diminished by reason of vulnerability'.[142] Additionally, the parties have to consider 'whether the quality of the evidence given by a party or witness is likely to be diminished by reason of vulnerability'.[143]

There are practical measures the Practical Guidance advise that may be relevant and available:

- Prevent a party or witness from seeing or being seen by another party or witness (such as screens).

- Allow party or witness to participate in hearings and give evidence from another location by live link (such as Skype or video conferencing or telephone.

- Provide for a party or witness to use a device to help communication.

- Provide for a party or witness to participate in proceedings with the assistance of an intermediary (such as a communication specialist or British Sign Language interpreter).

- Provide for a party or witness to be questioned in tribunal with the assistance of an intermediary.[144]

---

[141] ibid, para 14.

[142] ibid, para 6.

[143] ibid, para 6.

[144] ibid, para 15.

The Presidential Guidance states, 'both the Criminal Procedure Rules and the Family Procedure Rules make specific provision for vulnerable parties and witnesses'.[145] There is no need to 'reinvent the wheel if the excellent work done in the criminal, family and civil jurisdictions can be adapted for use in the Employment Tribunal'.[146]

[145] ibid, para 12.

[146] ibid.

CHAPTER EIGHT

VULNERABLE WITNESSES IN PERSONAL INJURY PROCEEDINGS

Personal injury lawyers making claims for witnesses often represent people who are fearful and traumatised. Both defendants and claimants can be vulnerable, thus it is the justice system's duty to be inclusive those who participate in it.

The most recent organ of government to consider the vulnerability of people and the civil justice needing change is The Civil Procedure Rules Committee. It strongly advocates for change with support from the Civil Justice Council, the Independent Inquiry into Child Sexual Abuse and the Ministry of Justice.[147] The case for reform is significant is because the Civil Justice System lacks development in comparison to the Criminal and Family systems, in the way they deal with vulnerable witnesses.[148] The Civil Courts have not been under an obligation to consider the vulnerability of witnesses. The Civil Court argues it has the power to assist witnesses, by virtue of the objective 1.1 of the Criminal Procedure Rules (CPR).[149] However, to get the Court to use this power is a challenge. The Court has to take into consideration:

---

[147] Jonathan Wheeler, 'Vulnerable Witnesses – Setting the Ground Rules' (*BoltBurdonKemp*, 17 September 2020) <https://www.boltburdonkemp.co.uk/our-insights/vulnerable-witnesses-setting-the-ground-rules/#fn10>

accessed 12 August 2021.

[148] ibid.

[149] The Criminal Procedure Rules 2020, pt 1.1.

- The Court's power of case management under CPR 1.4[150] and 3.1(2)(m);[151]
- Hearing oral evidence by video link under CPR 32.3;[152] or
- By deposition under CPR 34.8;[153] or
- Excluding the identity of a witness by being kept private, under CPR 39.2(4).[154]

In the Civil Courts, Judges have allowed the use of screen to give evidence; allowing a witness to use a private room as a waiting room and facilitated different entering and exiting routes.

The claimant in the personal injury case, *Connor v Castle Cement*[155] had permission to rely on an intermediary, giving him assistance during his oral testimony. The claimant was suffering from a chronic psychological condition, related to dementia.

It is for the Judge to decide whether special measures are applicable and if ordered, the Court must put in place the resources to assist the witness. Additionally, Civil Judges must consider the vulnerability of witnesses during the first case management stage.

There are circumstances where personal injury lawyers are most concerned:

---

150 The Criminal Procedure Rules 2020 pt 1.4.

151 The Criminal Procedure Rules 2020 pt 3.2(1)(m).

152 The Criminal Procedure Rules 2020 pt 32.3.

153 The Criminal Procedure Rules 2020 pt 34.8.

154 The Criminal Procedure Rules 2020 pt 39.2(4).

155 *Connor v Castle Cement* [2016] EWHC 300 (QB).

- A vicious cross-examination of a vulnerable witness, whereby the judge has failed to intervene;[156]

- the client's abuser was allowed to cross-examine him/her directly, although they have been convicted of crimes against him/her;[157]

- in a different, two witnesses were questioned on facts of their abuse, after the defence counsel had explained the facts prior;[158]

- lawyers have been instructed by a client/clients to take a low offer, avoiding the trauma of giving evidence in Court.[159]

The Civil Justice Council

The Civil Justice Council in an advisory public body. It was established to coordinate the modernisation of the civil justice system. The Ministry of Justice asked the Council to evaluate the system, regarding vulnerable witnesses in the Civil Courts. The Ministry of Justice requested this, after the publication of the Independent Inquiry into Child Sexual Abuse's report in 2018. The inquiry highlighted the inequality between the criminal and civil justice system where vulnerable witnesses were concerned. The Civil Procedure Rules Committee recommended the rules be amended "to ensure that Judges presiding over cases relating to child sexual abuse consider the use of protections for vulnerable witnesses".[160] The issues raised where not subject to sufficient focus and

[156] Jonathan Wheeler, 'Vulnerable Witnesses – Setting the Ground Rules' (*BoltBurdonKemp*, 17 September 2020) <https://www.boltburdonkemp.co.uk/our-insights/vulnerable-witnesses-setting-the-ground-rules/#fn10> accessed 12 August 2021.

[157] ibid.

[158] ibid.

[159] ibid.

[160] IICSA Interim Report (25 April 2018) <https://www.iicsa.org.uk/document/full-interim-report-independent-inquiry-child-sexual-abuse> accessed 12 August 2021.

thus, the actions taken were not applied consistently. The Civil Justice Council in 2020 suggested a list of recommendations to facilitate reform in civil cases. The Court would have to consider the vulnerability of witnesses during the early stages of a case. The witnesses should be notified of any issues during the direction questionnaire stage.

The Civil Justice Council exemplified:

- the importance of training judges and court staff to deal with vulnerable witnesses giving the best evidence possible. Similar profession bodies also need to educate their employees.

- the Civil Courts must adopt the resources ruled by the Judge's direction. This could include screens, video-link facilities, private waiting rooms, and separate ways of entering or exiting the court room. Special consideration must be given to intermediaries and interpreters, used by people whose first language is not English.

- the power to prohibit the cross examination of a vulnerable witness by a perpetrator is up to the Judge. The Court has the power and must appoint a lawyer to conduct cross examination on behalf of a litigant, paid by public funds.

The Civil Procedure Rules Committee

The role of the committee is to bring existing powers under one scope. On the 15th of May 2020, the committee discussed the following issues:

- Does the over-riding objective need to be amended to accommodate the focus on vulnerability?

- Does vulnerability need to be defined?

- Does the concept of proportionality be amended?

- Will fixed costs regimes need to be changed to accommodate additional work to assist vulnerable witnesses?

Ensuring vulnerability is the priority in the Court system has involved the Civil Procedure Rules Committee amending the over-riding objective. This is to ensure witnesses have an equal footing and can "fully participate in the proceedings" so they "can give their best evidence". A list of factors should be considered when assessing whether a witness is vulnerable. The factors below may determine if a witness or party is vulnerable and is "not limited to:

- age, maturity or lack of understanding;
- communication or language difficulties (including literacy);
- physical disability or disorder;
- mental disorder or significant impairment of intelligence or social functioning (including learning difficulties);
- the subject matter of, or facts relevant to, the case or the relationship with a party or witness (examples: sexual assault, domestic violence or intimidation (actual or perceived));
- social or domestic circumstances, cultural background or ethnic origins".[161]

The committee proposed these factors be implemented into the new practice direction. The Court would have to consider a person's vulnerability and the impact of questioning them. The issues would have to be considering at the earliest stages of the case; determining which measures can be used in court, to facilitate the vulnerable witness. For these changes to be successfully implemented, additional changes will need to be made regarding cost allocations. This is defined at 44.3(4) CPR,[162] "any additional work or expense incurred due to the

[161] Civil Justice Council, 'Vulnerable Witnesses and Parties Within Civil Proceedings: Current Position and Recommendations for Change' (20 February 2020) para 185.

[162] The Criminal Procedure Rules 2020, pt 44.3(4).

vulnerability of a party or any witness".[163] Flexibility with fixed recoverable costs is also needed for the purpose of vulnerable witnesses.[164]

163 *Connor v Castle Cement [*2016] EWHC 300 (QB).

164 Civil Justice Council, 'Vulnerable Witnesses and Parties Within Civil Proceedings: Current Position and Recommendations for Change' (20 February 2020) para 233.

CHAPTER NINE

VULNERABLE WITNESSES IN OTHER COUNTRIES AND JURISDICTIONS

I have sought to outline just some of the jurisdictions. It is not all. If you appear in some of these jurisdictions, then please feel free to share with me what works and what does not work.

As a busy barrister at law, I cannot claim to have the knowledge of every jurisdiction but here I outline some of the ones I have experience of or advice in.

MONTSERRAT

The Montserrat Family Protection Against Domestic Violence Act[165] outlines "special measures in case of vulnerable witnesses:

> **19.**(1) Where during the receipt of evidence from a witness in any proceedings under this Act it appears to the Court that the witness is vulnerable, the Court may take such measures as it considers necessary in the circumstances to safeguard the integrity of the evidence being given by that witness.
>
> (2) The measures which may be taken by the Court under subsection (1) include –
>
> *(a)* permitting the video recording of the evidence;

[165] Montserrat Family Protection Against Domestic Violence Act 2002.

(b) permitting cross examination of the witness over video link or with the use of screens; and

(c) preventing the personal cross-examination of the witness by the defendant.

(3) For the purposes of this section a witness is vulnerable if for any reason peculiar to the witness or the circumstances, it appears to the Court that the integrity of the evidence will be affected if special measures are not taken to safeguard the integrity of such evidence".

The Criminal Procedure Code of Montserrat, No.9 of 2010[166] differs from the family provisions. Part 32 of the Criminal Procedure Code[167] outlines the vulnerable and intimidated witnesses special measures. Under Part 32(1) an 'eligible witness' means a "witness eligible for assistance by virtue of Section 270 or 271".[168] The definition of 'live link' means a "television or other arrangement whereby a witness, while absent from the courtroom or other place where the proceedings are being held, is able to see and hear a person there and to be seen and heard by the persons specified in Section 227(2)(a) to (c)". The 'quality' of "evidence of a witness, shall be construed in accordance with 270(5)".

Witnesses eligible for assistance on grounds of age or incapacity are under Section 270:

(1) "For the purposes of this Part, a witness in criminal proceedings (other than the accused) is eligible for assistance by virtue of this section –

(a) if under the age of 17 at the time of the hearing; or

166 Criminal Procedure Code of Montserrat No.9 of 2010.

167 Criminal Procedure Code of Montserrat No.9 of 2010, pt 32.

168 Criminal Procedure Code of Montserrat No.9 of 2010, pt 32(1).

(b) if the court considers that the quality of evidence given by the witness is likely to be diminished by reason of any circumstances falling within subsection (2).

(2) The circumstances falling within this subsection are –

(a) that the witness –

(i) is of unsound mind within the meaning of the Mental Treatment Act, or

(ii) otherwise has a significant impairment of intelligence and social functioning;

(b) that the witness has a physical disability or is suffering from a physical disorder".[169]

Whether any special measure or measures are to be improved or maximise practicability, the quality of evidence given by the witness, the Court must consider all circumstances of the case:

(a) "any views expressed by the witness; and

(b) whether the measure or measures might tend to inhibit such evidence being effectively tested by a party to the proceedings".[170]

Under Section 273(4), provisions in a special measures direction must specify the special measure, applicable to the witness's evidence.[171] Section 273(5) exemplifies nothing under Section 273 will not affect the power of the Court to make an order or give leave:

(a) "in relation to a witness who is not eligible witness; or

---

[169] Criminal Procedure Code of Montserrat No.9 of 2010, s 270.

[170] ibid.

[171] Criminal Procedure Code of Montserrat No.9 of 2010, s 273(4).

(b) in relation to an eligible witness where (as, for example, in a case where a foreign language interpreter is to be provided) the order is made or leave is given otherwise than by reason of the fact that the witness is an eligible witness".[172]

Section 275 outlines the special provisions relating to child witnesses.[173] Section 275(1)(a) defines a 'child witness', "if he is an eligible witness by reason of Section 270(1)(a)".[174]

A child witness is allowed 'special protection' if the offence is of a sexual nature or other specific circumstances listed in Parts XII, XIII or XIV of the Penal Code. Additionally, a 'relevant recording', including a video recording interview can be made of a child witness, if it is to be admitted as evidence-in-chief.

Under Section 275(3), the Court must give a special measures direction regarding a child witness, complying with:

(a) "it must provide for any relevant recording to be admitted under section 281 (video recorded evidence in chief); and

(b) it must provide for any evidence given by the witness in the proceedings which is not given by means of a video recording (whether in chief or otherwise) to be given by means of a live link in accordance with section 278".[175]

Section 276 is an extension of the provision above, regarding witnesses over the age of 17.[176] The same rules apply in relation to special measures and giving video evidence.

---

[172] Criminal Procedure Code of Montserrat No.9 of 2010, s 273(5).

[173] Criminal Procedure Code of Montserrat No.9 of 2010, s 275.

[174] Criminal Procedure Code of Montserrat No.9 of 2010, s 275(1)(a).

[175] Criminal Procedure Code of Montserrat No.9 of 2010, s 275(3).

[176] Criminal Procedure Code of Montserrat No.9 of 2010, s 276.

The special measures applicable under the **Criminal Procedure Code, in Montserrat** include:

- Screening witness from accused
- Evidence by live link
- Evidence given in private
- Removal of gowns
- Video recorded evidence in chief
- Video recorded cross-examination or re-examination
- Examination of witness through intermediary
- Aid to communication

Screening witness from accused

Section 277(1) states screening a witness from an accused is a special measures direction. This provide witnesses, giving a testimony or being sworn in court, protection from being seen by the accused.[177] Under Section 277(2), the screen must not prevent the witness from being able to see and be seen by:

(a) "the judge or justices (or both) and the jury (if there is one);

(b) legal representatives acting in the proceedings; and

(c) any interpreter or other person appointed (in pursuance of the direction or otherwise) to assist the witness".[178]

177 Criminal Procedure Code of Montserrat No.9 of 2010, s 277(1).

178 Criminal Procedure Code of Montserrat No.9 of 2010, s 277(2).

If there are more than one legal representative acting for a party, the witness must be able to see at least one of them.

Evidence by live link

Section 278(1)[179] permits evidence to be given by live link. If permission is given to use live link as a means of giving evidence, other methods should not be used – unless there is permission from the Court. The Court may give their permission to use other methods, if it is in the interests of justice to do so and if there has been material change of circumstances.

If there are proceedings in a Magistrates' Court:

(a) "evidence is to be given by means of a live link in accordance with a special measures direction, but

(b) Suitable facilities for receiving such evidence are not available at the court-house in which that court can (apart from this subsection) lawfully sit, the Court may sit for the purposes of the whole or any part of those proceedings at a place where such facilities are available and which has been appointed for the purposes of this subsection by the justices acting for the petty sessions area for which the court acts".[180]

Evidence given in private

Section 279 allows evidence to be given in private, if it does not include:

(2)(a) "the accused,

(b) legal representatives acting in the proceedings, or

179 Criminal Procedure Code of Montserrat No.9 of 2010, s 278(1).

180 ibid.

(c) any interpreter or other person appointed (in pursuance of the direction or otherwise) to assist the witness".[181]

Section 279(3) states "for representatives of news gathering or reporting organisations to be so excluded shall be expressed not to apply to one named person who –

(a) is a representative of such an organisation, and

(b) has been nominated for the purpose by one or more such organisations,

unless it appears to the Court that no such nomination has been made".[182]

Removal of gowns

Whilst the witness is giving evidence, the special measures direction permits the removal of gowns.

Video recorded evidence in chief

Video recorded evidence in chief is permitted under Section 281(4)(a) if it appears to the Court:

(i) "the witness will not be available for cross-examination (whether conducted in the ordinary way or in accordance with any such direction), and

(ii) the parties to the proceedings have not agreed that there is no need for the witness to be so available".[183]

Under the same Section, subsection 5, a recording is admitted if:

---

[181] Criminal Procedure Code of Montserrat No.9 of 2010, s 279.

[182] Criminal Procedure Code of Montserrat No.9 of 2010, s 279(3).

[183] Criminal Procedure Code of Montserrat No.9 of 2010, s 281(4)(a).

(a) "the witness must be called by the party tendering it in evidence, unless –

(i) a special measures direction provides for the witness's evidence on cross-examination to be given otherwise than by testimony in court, or

(ii) the parties to the proceedings have agreed as mentioned in subsection (4)(a)(ii); and

(b) the witness may not give evidence in chief otherwise than by means of the recording –

(i) as to many matter which, in the opinion of the Court, has been dealt with adequately in the witness's recorded testimony, or

(ii) without the permission of the Court, as to any other matter which, in the opinion of the Court, is dealt with in that testimony".[184]

Video recorded cross-examination or re-examination

Where video recordings are admitted under Section 281[185] as evidence in chief, Section 282[186] provides for any cross-examination and re-examination of a witness by video recording.

The recording must be made in the presence of the Judge, Magistrate or legal representative acting in the proceedings. They must be able to see and hear the examination of the witness, in the presence of the recording being made.

Where a recording has been made, examining a witness, the witness may not be cross-examined or re-examined in relation to the evidence given

184 Criminal Procedure Code of Montserrat No.9 of 2010, s 281(5).

185 Criminal Procedure Code of Montserrat No.9 of 2010, s 281.

186 Criminal Procedure Code of Montserrat No.9 of 2010, s 282.

by the evidence in the proceedings. Only if the Court has given permission, with a further special measures direction, can another cross-examination or re-examination take place. The Court may give a further direction if there is uncertainty regarding the cross-examination made on video or it is in the interests of justice.

Examination of witness through intermediary

Under Section 283(1)[187] an intermediary is an interpreter or other person approved by the Court. Section 283(2) outlines the "function of an intermediary is to communicate –

(a) to the witness, questions put to the witness, and

(b) to any person asking such questions, the answers given by the witness in reply to them,

and to explain such questions or answers so far as necessary to enable them to be understood by the witness or person in question".[188]

Section 283(7) states an intermediary can be liable for perjury in a judicial proceeding if they act unlawfully.[189] They have a duty to uphold the law and act lawfully whilst assisting a witness.

Aids to communication

Devices which the Court considers appropriate to enable questions and answers to be communicated with, can be used in Court under Section 284.[190] These devices can assist any disability, disorder or other impairments which the witness may suffer from.

187 Criminal Procedure Code of Montserrat No.9 of 2010, s 283(1).

188 Criminal Procedure Code of Montserrat No.9 of 2010, s 283(2).

189 Criminal Procedure Code of Montserrat No.9 of 2010, s 283(7).

190 Criminal Procedure Code of Montserrat No.9 of 2010, s 284.

AUSTRALIA

Laws in Australia are made at state and federal level.[191] It is important to understand this for context. States have their own system of Courts and Tribunals to administer state laws.[192] National laws are made by the Federal Government, operating nationally and overlaying the legal framework created by state laws.[193]

A witness will give evidence in the courtroom. In **criminal cases**, there are special provisions available to assist vulnerable witnesses.

The provisions include children and people with cognitive impairments. The "special provisions:

- Having a friend or relative in court while you give evidence, provided that this support person is not also appearing as a witness;
- Having a screen in the court, so you do not have to see the accused while you give evidence;
- Having the court closed to the public while you give evidence;
- Giving your evidence on closed circuit television".[194]

Prosecutors can apply to the court for the use of special provisions, on behalf of vulnerable witnesses. It is for the Judge or Magistrate to grant permission for their use.

---

[191] Other Australian Courts, 'Other Australian Courts' (Court Services Victoria, 12 February 2020) <https://www.courts.vic.gov.au/court-system/other-australian-courts> accessed 15 August 2021.

[192] ibid.

[193] ibid.

[194] ibid.

The South Australian Evidence Act 1929[195] states special arrangements can be made for 'vulnerable' witnesses. The Act protects vulnerable witnesses from:

- Distress or embarrassment,
- Intimidation from the courtroom atmosphere, or
- Any other proper reason.

The Statutes Amendment Evidence and Procedure Act 2008 defines "vulnerable witness as:

a) a witness who is under 16 years of age; or

b) a witness who suffers from a mental disability; or

c) a witness who is the alleged victim of an offence to which the proceedings relate –

i) where the offence is a serious offence against the person; or

ii) in any other case – where, because of the circumstances of the witness or the circumstances of the case, the witness would, in the opinion of the court, be specially disadvantaged if not treated as a vulnerable witness; or

d) a witness who –

i) has been subjected to threats of violence or retribution in connection with the proceedings; or

[195] South Australian Evidence Act 1929.

ii) has reasonable grounds to fear violence or retribution in connection with the proceedings".[196]

Vulnerable Witness Provisions:

The Evidence Act 1929 Vulnerable Witness Provisions[197] include:

Closed Circuit Television (CCTV)

The closed-circuit television allows witnesses to give evidence from a separate room. It is transmitted to the courtroom via CCTV. Those present in Court can hear the witness on the TV screens in the courtroom. The witness will be able to see and hear the lawyers, also the Judge asking questions. The vulnerable witness will not see the accused on the screen.

One Way Screen

The screen is placed between the vulnerable witness and the accused, blocking the view of them. The screen acts as a one-way barrier; the accused can see the vulnerable witness giving evidence.

Court companion

The allows the vulnerable witness to be accompanied by a volunteer, friend, family member or social worker. Their duty is to give supportive physical presence, whilst the witness gives evidence. They must not be involved with the case, talk or assistance giving evidence. The Judge and Jury must be able to see the Court companion while the witness gives evidence.

Closed Court

An application can be made to Court, to bar members of the public from watching in the public gallery. This is granted in circumstances where the

[196] Statutes Amendment Evidence and Procedure Act 2008.

[197] Evidence Act 1929 Vulnerable Witness Provisions.

evidence is sensitive, personal or embarrassing. The Close Court provision prevents people who are not known to the vulnerable witness from watching them give evidence.

Applications for the Vulnerable Witnesses Provisions need to be filed to the Court at the earliest stage possible. This must occur before the trial begins. Within 14 days of the request being filed with the Court, the request must be given to the accused. There are some situations where witnesses can make late requests, however there is no guarantee the application will be granted.

TASMANIA

On the 1st of March 2021, the Tasmanian Government announced the introduction of a landmark pilot scheme. The scheme would ensure children and vulnerable witnesses would be supported, being able to participate in the Tasmanian criminal justice system effectively.

(I was interviewed by Professor Penny Cooper for a podcast from a practitioner's view in the UK). Professor Cooper has been advising The Tasmanian government on the scheme.

The Pilot Intermediary Scheme will enable experts to act as witness intermediaries, in Tasmanian Courts. Lawyers, Judges and intermediaries will work together, to assist children and witnesses who have communication needs.

The scheme was established after recommendations of the Royal Commission into Institutional Responses to Child Sexual Abuse in its Criminal Justice Report and the 2018 report of the Tasmanian Law Reform Institute.

The Attorney General and Minister for Justice announced 23 qualified professionals with specialist skills in communication completed their training, prior to the launch of the pilot scheme. The introduction of the scheme is a demonstration of the Tasmanian's Government commitment to ensuring citizens have access to justice, during stressful and turbulent times.

The Tasmanian Parliament on the 25th of August 2020 introduced the Evidence Children and Special Witnesses Amendment Bill 2020. On the 15th of September, the Bill reached the first stage in the Legislative Council. The Bill amends the Evidence Children and Special Witnesses Act 2001 (TAS),[198] the Criminal Code Act 1924 (TAS)[199] and the Legal Aid Commission Act 1990 (TAS).[200] The purpose was to establish a legislative framework of the use of intermediaries in Tasmanian Courts.

The Bill amends the Evidence Children and Special Witnesses Act 2001 to:

- "Define the scope of the Pilot Intermediary Scheme to apply to:
    - all children under the age of 18 years participating in the criminal justice process who are victims or witnesses (other than a defendant) in sexual offence matters and/or matters under Chapter XVII of the Criminal Code Act 1924; and
    - adults with a communication need participating in the criminal justice process who are victims or witnesses (other than a defendant) in sexual offence matters and/or matters under Chapter XVII of the Criminal Code Act 1924.
- Define 'communication need' applicable to adult victims and witnesses;
- Require the Secretary of the Department of Justice to establish and maintain a panel of persons who the Secretary considers are suitable to be witness intermediaries, the Intermediaries Panel;

---

198 Evidence Children and Special Witnesses Act 2001 (TAS).

199 Criminal Code Act 1924 (TAS).

200 Legal Aid Commission Act 1990 (TAS).

- Provide for the Secretary of the Department of Justice to allocate a person from the Intermediaries Panel to perform the relevant functions of a witness intermediary in respect of a witness;
- Set out the functions of a witness intermediary, including providing an assessment report and providing recommendations during a specified proceeding the Judge, and any Lawyer appearing in the proceeding as to adjustments to be made in the proceeding;
- Require a person to take an oath or affirmation before acting as a witness intermediary in specified proceedings in a court;
- Provide for the circumstances in which a Judge is to make an order an assessment report be prepared.
- Give a Judge the power to make an order that a witness intermediary be used in respect of a witness in a specified proceeding, if having considered an assessment report, the Judge is satisfied that the use of a witness intermediary will assist proceedings (a Witness Intermediary Order);
- Give a prescribed witness the same rights as an 'affected person' and 'affected child' under the Act.
- Provide that a Judge must direct that a ground rules hearings be held for a prescribed witness in a specified proceeding and provides that a Judge may make directions in a ground rules hearing;
- Amend section 8A to prevent a defendant directly cross-examining a prescribed witness unless the cross-examination is undertaken by counsel;
- Clarify that a Judge may make an order under section 8A(3) directing that an unrepresented defendant be given assistance

under the Legal Aid Commission Act 1990 for cross-examination only if it's in the interests of justice to do so;

- Require the Legal Aid Commission to provide legal aid for the purpose of cross-examining the witness or person, without applying the income, assets or other merits test".[201]

Witness *intermediaries* will be **neutral officers** of the Court. They will support the Prosecution and Defence lawyers to ensure vulnerable witnesses will feel comfortable. Their role is to make sure the witnesses have access to the materials, time and space they need to communicate their best evidence. The role of an intermediary is impartial and they have a duty to reduce the rates of re-traumatisation associated to the justice system.

An **intermediary** has an active role in the criminal justice system and will:

- "assess a vulnerable witness' communication needs prior to the police interview and be present during the interview;
- provide oral recommendations to the police about how best to communicate with a vulnerable witness;
- prepare reports for the Courts providing advice about witnesses' comprehension and communication capacities;
- identify appropriate and inappropriate styles of questioning;
- identify any special measures or facilities that might be needed;
- advise Counsel on the wording of the proposed questions;

[201] Evidence Children and Special Witnesses Act 2001.

- sit with the witness during the trial process and alert the Court to any problematic use of questioning or concerns about fatigue or distress".[202]

CHILE

The former Chilean Criminal Procedure was established on an inquisitorial process. Since then, reform has shaped the social, political, economic and cultural developments in Chile. Different institutions deal with separate areas of investigations, guaranteeing the impartiality of Judges and transparency of the Court process.

The main institutions are:

- The Public Ministry – The role of the Public Ministry is to investigate crime; prosecuting individuals responsible. This institution is under the control of the Attorney General, who instruct the attorneys at national level.

- The Criminal Public Defender – The Criminal Public Defender is responsible for providing free legal defense to those who have been prosecuted. The purpose of this organisation is to ensure there is a professional service available to all, regardless of the crime they are being prosecuted for.

- The Supervisory Judge – The Judge specialises in criminal law and in charge of the investigating process. The Judge has the duty to protect rights of all the people involved in the judicial process. This includes those being prosecuted, victims and witnesses.

---

[202] Marita O'Connell, 'Witness Intermediaries Occupational Therapy Australia Handout' (Department of Justice Child Abuse Royal Commission Response Unit, September 2020) <https://otaus.com.au/publicassets/eae7c455-55fd-ea11-9434-005056be13b5/Intermediary%20Information%20for%20OT%20Aus%20%201.pdf > accessed 15 August 2021.

Structure of the courts

There is a hierarchical structure amongst Chilean Courts. The Supreme Court is at the top, followed by 17 Courts of Appeal. They have jurisdiction over several lower Civil Courts. The lower Civil Courts have jurisdiction over different matters. The Courts of Appeal have the duty of rulings over appeals. The Supreme Court is in charge of ruling higher appeals and disciplinary recourses filed against the rulings in the Courts of Appeal. In addition to its duties, the Supreme Court also supervises the administrative, economic and disciplinary aspects of the lower Courts.

In Chile, there are different protection measures for felony and non-felony cases. Measures include keeping the identity of witnesses private; protective incarceration; relocation and identity change. Other protections measures can be police patrols, changing telephone numbers and other common measures. A Prosecutor or Court can request the police to apply these measures. In criminal investigations, only witnesses can refused to answer a question based on the privilege against professional secrecy, self-incrimination and incrimination of a close relative.

Court room dogs in Chile

As a dog lover myself, I am pleased to see the use of dogs in the court room in Chile.

In addition, Chile allows the use of courthouse dogs. They are expertly trained canines, assisting individuals with psychological, emotional or physical difficulties.[203] They provide companionship and comfort, accompanying the vulnerable witness during in-court testimonies and interviews.[204] The dogs are increasingly used to assist young vulnerable

[203] Kayla Burd and Dawn Mcquiston, 'Facility Dogs in the Courtroom: Comfort Without Prejudice?' (2019) 44(4) CJR 1.

[204] ibid.

witnesses in Court, as well as disabled witnesses and the elderly.[205] According to the Courthouse Dogs Foundation, there are approximately 200 facility dogs working across 40 states in America, Canada and Chile.[206] When in Court, the dog lies beside the witness, on the floor. In some instances, the dog is hidden from the juror's view entirely. It is no surprise the legal system has implemented the use of support dogs. The achievement has been significant, with the dogs ultimately assisting alleged abuse complainants in seeking justice.[207]

The most significant improvement regarding Chile's judicial system is the application of law.

This incorporates impartiality, transparency, immediate appreciation of the evidence, rapid procedures, efficient management regarding resources available; due defence of the prosecuted; the protection the State grants to witnesses and victims; and the attention the State provides to help citizens overcome the consequences of crime.[208]

Chile still has many issues as country but on this issue much has been achieved.

Children accompanied by a therapy dog during an interview were significantly more likely to disclose abuse for substantiated cases. Thus, research should investigate whether these findings extrapolate to in-court testimony: Do facility dogs promote more effective communication for vulnerable witnesses and, thus, increased completeness of testimony compared to other accommodations? If

---

[205] ibid 2.

[206] David Crenshaw, Lori Stella, Ellen O'Neill-Stephens and Celeste Walsen, 'Developmentally and Trauma-Sensitive Courtrooms' (2016) 59(6) Journal of Humanistic Psychology 17.

[207] Kayla Burd and Dawn Mcquiston, 'Facility Dogs in the Courtroom: Comfort Without Prejudice?' (2019) 44(4) CJR 3.

[208] Sergio Endress Gómez, 'Essential Issues of the Chilean Legal System' (*GlobaLex*, November 2005) <https://www.nyulawglobal.org/globalex/Chile.html> accessed 17 August 2021.

facility dogs provide comfort without prejudice in court, it will be important for the legal system to consider those empirical findings as it moves forward in its treatment of and rulings concerning vulnerable witnesses and defendants in the courtroom.

Authors' Note

We thank Garrett Harris, Colin Hayton, Annamaria Hidalgo, Mason McCullough, and Cole Watson for their assistance with data collection. This research was presented at the 2017 meeting of the International Courthouse Dogs Foundation and the 2018 meeting of the American Psychological Association. Portions of this work are based on the first author's master's thesis, which was supported by the New College of Interdisciplinary Arts & Sciences, Arizona State University.

Declaration of Conflicting Interests

The authors declared no potential conflicts of interest with respect to the research, authorship, and/or publication of this article.

Funding

The authors received no financial support for the research, authorship, and/or publication of this article.

ORCID iD

Kayla A. Burd https://orcid.org/0000-0002-0107-8788

References

Berry, A., Borgi, M., Francia, N., Alleva, E., & Cirulli, F. (2013). Use of assistance and therapy dogs for children with autism spectrum disorders: A critical review of the current evidence. The Journal of Alternative and Complementary Medicine, 19, 73–80. doi:10.1089/acm.2011.0835

Bornstein, B. H. (1999). The ecological validity of jury simulations: Is the jury still out? Law and Human Behavior, 23, 75–91.

Bowers, S. V. (2013). The use of "therapy dogs" in Indiana courtrooms: Why a dog might not be a defendant's best friend. Indiana Law Review, 46, 1289–1315.

Bradley, P. (2014). Therapy dogs in the courtroom as advocates for child witnesses: An interpretive phenomenological analysis of judges' opinions, experiences, and rulings (Unpublished doctoral dissertation). Texas A&M University–Commerce, Commerce.

Bright, D. A., & Goodman-Delahunty, J. (2006). Gruesome evidence and emotion: Anger, blame, and jury decision-making. Law and Human Behavior, 30, 183–202. Cacioppo, J. T., Petty, R. E., & Kao, C. F. (1984). The efficient assessment of need for cognition. Journal of Personality Assessment, 48, 306–307. doi:10.1207/s15327752jpa4803_13

Cacioppo, J. T., Petty, R. E., & Kao, C. F. (1984). The efficient assessment of need for cognition. Journal of Personality Assessment, 48, 306–307. doi:10.1207/s15327752jpa4803_13

Crenshaw, D. A., Stella, L., O'Neill-Stephens, E., & Walsen, C. (2016). Developmentally and trauma-sensitive courtrooms. Journal of Humanistic Psychology, 1–17. doi:10.1177/0022167816641854

Dellinger, M. (2009). Using dogs for emotional support of testifying victims of crime.

CHAPTER TEN

PRACTICAL THINGS TO THINK ABOUT

In a post Covid-19 world with a huge amount of backlogs in the criminal justice system, with cases with vulnerable witnesses and defendants being a priority. However with pressures on the criminal justice system, on judges and courts staff and barrister, planning has never been more important.

One can see why judges would be concerned and even angry at late application for the use of intermediaries. They inevitable make trials longer and with already pressured trial lists it important to the following:

a. Do consider the use of intermediaries

b. Have early conferences to determine this.

c. Some vulnerabilities are more obvious than others. Young black boys who cannot spell?

d. Expelled offenders from school (Lammy report).

e. Alert the court preferably at PTPH

f. Keep the court listing and Judge abreast of having difficulties involving intermediaries especially and including finding an expert to write a report.

g. Ensure the expert report does not cover instructions given by the defendant covering the offence.

h. Instructions about the offence are covered by privilege

i. Keep an eye on costs to the public purse whilst ensuring fair trial and access to justice.

j. Remind Judges of the case law if struggling with judges who question the use of intermediaries.

k. Remind judges and have recent court of appeal decisions to hand.

l. Encourage experts to use the technologies now available to interview the vulnerable person. Including accused persons. Skype, Zoom, CVP are all permissible especially in getting earlier reports.

m. Submit questions for intermediaries especially where young and vulnerable children are concerned early.

n. Keep trials on the road –

Consider, early case summaries and opening is you are prosecuting for the Crown.

If defending submit, early defence case summaries, video edits, ABE and ROTI (record of interview) edits.

o. Keep courts and judges informed. List the case for case management or PTR or Mention if issues arise

p. We can all have a number of trials and cases at a time. Don't leave these issues to the last minute.

q. Justice must not only be done buy must be seen to be done .

r. Good luck with your trial.

CHAPTER ELEVEN

CONCLUSION

To assist vulnerable persons, I often take the characters from a children's book I have written.

Rosie and the unicorn. The characters have been knitted and includes a barrister at Law, circuit judge, and so on.

The next book shows what happens when you go to court. The books are beautifully illustrated.

It might be a good distraction for children waiting at court to give evidence to learn about what the court process will entail. What the judge might look like.

Intermediaries often contact me for the dolls from the book. Or the colouring in book.

Links to Rosie and the Unicorn Activity books are available at www.sallypenniauthor.co.uk

RESOURCES AND FURTHER READING

In the writing of this book, I have found the following resources immensely useful.

I suggest you also read them.

Articles

https://www.counselmagazine.co.uk/articles/therapy-animals-and-abe

Resources and Further reading

Lots of **free resources, for example**

- Many articles/ blogs etc. on website

http://pennycooper.co.uk/publications/

- The Advocate's Gateway

https://www.theadvocatesgateway.org

ET Judge Brian Doyle, then President of the Employment Tribunals in England and Wales, on BBC Radio 4's Law in Action, March 2020. With Joshua Rosenburg.

Research and References

'Achieving Best Evidence in Criminal Proceedings': Ministry of Justice (March 2011).

'Achieving justice for defendants and witnesses with mental distress: A mental health toolkit for prosecutors and advocates' (MIND).

'Access to health records': BMA. 'Adult Psychiatric Morbidity Survey: Survey of Mental Health and Wellbeing, 2014': NHS Digital (29 September.2016).

Mental Disability Equal Treatment Bench Book 142 'Adverse Childhood Experiences and their association with chronic disease and health service use in the Welsh adult population': Public Health Wales NHS Trust (2016).

'Advocacy and the Vulnerable. National Training Programme. The 20 Principles of Questioning': The Inns of Court College of Advocacy (2019).

'Am I making myself clear? MENCAP's Guidelines for accessible writing'. 'Disability in the UK': Papworth Trust (2018).

'Care and support statutory guidance': Department of Health & Social Care (updated 24 June 2020).

'Code of Practice for Victims of Crime': MOJ (Nov 2020).

'Disability Rights in the UK – Updated submission to the UN Committee on the Rights of Persons with Disabilities in advance of the public examination of the UK's implementation of the UN CRPD': UK Independent Mechanism (July 2017).

'The Equality Act 2010: The impact on disabled people': House of Lords Select Committee on the Equality Act 2010 and Disability (2016).

'Great Expectations: Towards better learning outcomes for young people and young adults in custody': Prisoners' Education Trust (2016: 4).

'Guidance: Ex-armed service personnel in prison and on probation' (15 May 2019). 'The mental health of the UK armed forces' (Kings Centre for Military Health Research 2014). 'The Mental health of the UK Armed Forces' King's Centre for Military Health Research: Briefing Note (Sept 2018).

'Guidance on the use of s.28 YJCEA 1999; pre-recording of cross-examination and re-examination. For witnesses captured by s.17(4) YJCEA 1999' (30 September 2019).

'Guidelines in relation to children giving evidence in family proceedings': Family Justice Council (2011).

'Half a Century of Change: The Evidence of Child Victims': Toulmin Lecture, King's College London (2013).

'Inclusive Justice: a system designed for all': Equality and Human Rights Commission (June 2020).

'Inclusive justice: a system designed for all. Interim evidence report. Video hearings and their impact on effective participation': EHRC (22 April 2020). 'Mental Health Act Statistics, Annual Figures, England 2018-2019': NHS Digital (29 October 2019).

'A joint inspection of the treatment of offenders with learning disabilities within the criminal justice system': HM Inspectorate of Probation (March 2015). 'Mental health and learning disabilities in the criminal courts: Information for magistrates, district judges and court staff': McConnell and Talbot (The Prison Reform Trust and Rethink Mental Illness. 2013).

'A Joint Inspection of the Treatment of Offenders with Learning Disabilities within the Criminal Justice System – Phase 1 From Arrest to Sentence': Criminal Justice Joint Inspection (2014). 'Joint inspection report on the experience of young victims and witnesses in the Criminal Justice System': HMCPSI and HMIC (2012). 'Judicial College Bench Checklist: Young Witness Cases' (2012).

'The Lammy Review: An independent review into the treatment of, and outcomes for, Black, Asian and Minority Ethnic individuals in the Criminal Justice System' (2017).

Mental Disability Equal Treatment Bench Book 143 'Mental Health in Prisons': National Audit Office (June 2017).

'NICE impact mental health': National Institute for Health and Care Excellence (March 2019). 'Perceived barriers to accessing mental health services among black and minority ethnic (BME) communities: a qualitative study in South East England': Memon and others. BMJ Open (2016).

'Presidential Guidance: Vulnerable parties and witnesses in Employment Tribunal proceedings' (April 2020).

'A Protocol between the National Police Chiefs' Council, the CPS and HMCTS to Expedite Cases Involving Witnesses under 10 Years' (2018).

'Provision of therapy for child witnesses prior to a criminal trial – practice guidance': CPS, Department of Health and Home Office (2001).

'Provision of therapy for vulnerable or intimidated adult witnesses prior to a criminal trial – practice guidance': CPS, Department of Health and Home Office (2001).

'Raising the Bar: The handling of vulnerable witnesses, victims and defendants in court': Advocacy Training Council (Mar 2011). 'Registered Intermediary Procedural Guidance': Ministry of Justice, (2019).

'Sentencing offenders with mental disorders, developmental disorders or neurological impairments': Sentencing Council Guideline (1 Oct 2020).

'Special measures in rape trials: Exploring the impact of screens, live links and video-recorded evidence on mock juror deliberation': Ellison and Munro (2012).

'Stigma and barriers to care in service leavers with mental health problems': KCMHR (2017). Cases Cases were relevant as at the date of publication.

'Surviving or Thriving? The state of the UK's mental health': Mental Health Foundation (2017). 'Thriving at work: The Stevenson/Farmer review of mental health and employers' (October 2017). 'UK Poverty 2019/20': Joseph Rowntree Foundation.

'Traumatic Brain Injury in the Prison Population' Guidance': HMPPS (Oct 2019). Veterans 'Call to mind: A framework for action. Findings from the review of veterans and family members mental and related health needs assessments' Final report Oct 2015. 'Former Members of the Armed Forces and the Criminal Justice System: A Review on behalf of the Secretary of State': Stephen Phillips QC MP (2014).

'The treatment of young adults in the criminal justice system': House of Commons Justice Committee (Oct 2016).

'Victims Strategy': HM Government (Sept 2018). 'View from the President's Chambers (16): Children and vulnerable witnesses – where are we?': Sir James Munby (Jan 2017). 'A Voice for the Voiceless: The Victims' Commissioner's Review into the Provision of Registered Intermediaries for Children and Vulnerable Victims and Witnesses' (January 2018).

'Vulnerable witnesses and parties – current position and recommendations for change': Civil Justice Council (Feb 2020). 'The Witness Charter: Standards of Care for Witnesses in the Criminal Justice System': MOJ (Dec 2013).

'What are health inequalities?': The King's Fund (18 February 2020). Mental health and criminal justice 'Community Sentence Treatment Requirements Protocol – Process evaluation report': Department of Health & Social Care (June 2019). 'Inclusive Justice: a system designed for all': Equality and Human Rights Commission (June 2020).

'Working Together to Safeguard Children: A guide to inter-agency working to safeguard and promote the welfare of children': HM Government (2018).

'Young adults in the criminal justice system': House of Commons Justice Committee (12 June 2018). 'Youth Court Bench Book'

Cases

AM (Afghanistan) v. SSHD [2017] EWCA Civ 1123 J & K and another [2019] EWCA Civ 5 JE v SSWP (PIP) [2020] UKUT 17 (AAC) Ms B v An NHS Hospital Trust [2002] EWHC 429 Mental Disability Equal Treatment Bench Book 144 R (on the application of King) v Isleworth Crown Court [2001] All ER (D) 48 (Jan)

R v Manning [2020] EWCA Crim 592

R v Montaut [2019] EWCA Crim 2252 Rackham v NHS Professionals Ltd UKEAT/0110/15 Re A (Children) (Remote Hearing: Care and Placement Orders) [2020] EWCA Civ 583 S (Vulnerable Parent: Intermediary) [2020] EWCA Civ 763 SC v The United Kingdom 60958/00 [2004] ECHR 263 SB (Vulnerable adult: credibility) Ghana [2019] UKUT 00398 Shui v University of Manchester and others UKEAT/2360/16

'Fundamental Dishonesty and QOCS in Personal Injury Proceedings: Law and Practice' by Jake Rowley
'A Practical Guide to the Law in Relation to School Exclusions' by Charlotte Hadfield & Alice de Coverley
'A Practical Guide to Divorce for the Silver Separators' by Karin Walker
'The Right to be Forgotten – The Law and Practical Issues' by Melissa Stock
'A Practical Guide to Planning Law and Rights of Way in National Parks, the Broads and AONBs' by James Maurici QC, James Neill et al
'A Practical Guide to Election Law' by Tom Tabori
'A Practical Guide to the Law in Relation to Surrogacy' by Andrew Powell
'A Practical Guide to Claims Arising from Fatal Accidents – 2nd Edition' by James Patience
'A Practical Guide to the Ownership of Employee Inventions – From Entitlement to Compensation' by James Tumbridge & Ashley Roughton
'A Practical Guide to Asbestos Claims' by Jonathan Owen & Gareth McAloon
'A Practical Guide to Stamp Duty Land Tax in England and Northern Ireland' by Suzanne O'Hara
'A Practical Guide to the Law of Farming Partnerships' by Philip Whitcomb
'Covid-19, Homeworking and the Law – The Essential Guide to Employment and GDPR Issues' by Forbes Solicitors
'Covid-19, Force Majeure and Frustration of Contracts – The Essential Guide' by Keith Markham
'Covid-19 and Criminal Law – The Essential Guide' by Ramya Nagesh
'Covid-19 and Family Law in England and Wales – The Essential Guide' by Safda Mahmood
'A Practical Guide to the Law of Unlawful Eviction and Harassment – 2nd Edition' by Stephanie Lovegrove
'Covid-19, Residential Property, Equity Release and Enfranchisement – The Essential Guide' by Paul Sams and Louise Uphill
'Covid-19, Brexit and the Law of Commercial Leases – The Essential Guide' by Mark Shelton
'A Practical Guide to Costs in Personal Injury Claims – 2nd Edition' by Matthew Hoe

'A Practical Guide to the General Data Protection Regulation (GDPR) – 2nd Edition' by Keith Markham
'Ellis on Credit Hire – Sixth Edition' by Aidan Ellis & Tim Kevan
'A Practical Guide to Working with Litigants in Person and McKenzie Friends in Family Cases' by Stuart Barlow
'Protecting Unregistered Brands: A Practical Guide to the Law of Passing Off' by Lorna Brazell
'A Practical Guide to Secondary Liability and Joint Enterprise Post-Jogee' by Joanne Cecil & James Mehigan
'A Practical Guide to the Pre-Action RTA Claims Protocol for Personal Injury Lawyers' by Antonia Ford
'A Practical Guide to Neighbour Disputes and the Law' by Alexander Walsh
'A Practical Guide to Forfeiture of Leases' by Mark Shelton
'A Practical Guide to Coercive Control for Legal Practitioners and Victims' by Rachel Horman
'A Practical Guide to Rights Over Airspace and Subsoil' by Daniel Gatty
'Tackling Disclosure in the Criminal Courts – A Practitioner's Guide' by Narita Bahra QC & Don Ramble
'A Practical Guide to the Law of Driverless Cars – Second Edition' by Alex Glassbrook, Emma Northey & Scarlett Milligan
'A Practical Guide to TOLATA Claims' by Greg Williams
'A Practical Guide to Elderly Law – 2nd Edition' by Justin Patten
'A Practical Guide to the Law of Prescription in Scotland' by Andrew Foyle
'A Practical Guide to the Construction and Rectification of Wills and Trust Instruments' by Edward Hewitt
'A Practical Guide to the Law of Bullying and Harassment in the Workplace' by Philip Hyland
'How to Be a Freelance Solicitor: A Practical Guide to the SRA-Regulated Freelance Solicitor Model' by Paul Bennett
'A Practical Guide to Prison Injury Claims' by Malcolm Johnson
'A Practical Guide to the Small Claims Track - 2nd Edition' by Dominic Bright
'A Practical Guide to Advising Clients at the Police Station' by Colin Stephen McKeown-Beaumont

'A Practical Guide to Antisocial Behaviour Injunctions' by Iain Wightwick
'Practical Mediation: A Guide for Mediators, Advocates, Advisers, Lawyers, and Students in Civil, Commercial, Business, Property, Workplace, and Employment Cases' by Jonathan Dingle with John Sephton
'The Mini-Pupillage Workbook' by David Boyle
'A Practical Guide to Crofting Law' by Brian Inkster
'A Practical Guide to Spousal Maintenance' by Liz Cowell
'A Practical Guide to the Law of Domain Names and Cybersquatting' by Andrew Clemson
'A Practical Guide to the Law of Gender Pay Gap Reporting' by Harini Iyengar
'A Practical Guide to the Rights of Grandparents in Children Proceedings' by Stuart Barlow
'NHS Whistleblowing and the Law' by Joseph England
'Employment Law and the Gig Economy' by Nigel Mackay & Annie Powell
'A Practical Guide to Noise Induced Hearing Loss (NIHL) Claims' by Andrew Mckie, Ian Skeate, Gareth McAloon
'An Introduction to Beauty Negligence Claims – A Practical Guide for the Personal Injury Practitioner' by Greg Almond
'Intercompany Agreements for Transfer Pricing Compliance' by Paul Sutton
'Zen and the Art of Mediation' by Martin Plowman
'A Practical Guide to the SRA Principles, Individual and Law Firm Codes of Conduct 2019 – What Every Law Firm Needs to Know' by Paul Bennett
'A Practical Guide to Adoption for Family Lawyers' by Graham Pegg
'A Practical Guide to Industrial Disease Claims' by Andrew Mckie & Ian Skeate
'A Practical Guide to Redundancy' by Philip Hyland
'A Practical Guide to Vicarious Liability' by Mariel Irvine
'A Practical Guide to Applications for Landlord's Consent and Variation of Leases' by Mark Shelton
'A Practical Guide to Relief from Sanctions Post-Mitchell and Denton' by Peter Causton
'A Practical Guide to Equity Release for Advisors' by Paul Sams
'A Practical Guide to Financial Services Claims' by Chris Hegarty

'The Law of Houses in Multiple Occupation: A Practical Guide to HMO Proceedings' by Julian Hunt

'Occupiers, Highways and Defective Premises Claims: A Practical Guide Post-Jackson – 2nd Edition' by Andrew Mckie

'A Practical Guide to Financial Ombudsman Service Claims' by Adam Temple & Robert Scrivenor

'A Practical Guide to Advising Schools on Employment Law' by Jonathan Holden

'A Practical Guide to Running Housing Disrepair and Cavity Wall Claims: 2nd Edition' by Andrew Mckie & Ian Skeate

'A Practical Guide to Holiday Sickness Claims – 2nd Edition' by Andrew Mckie & Ian Skeate

'Arguments and Tactics for Personal Injury and Clinical Negligence Claims' by Dorian Williams

'A Practical Guide to Drone Law' by Rufus Ballaster, Andrew Firman, Eleanor Clot

'A Practical Guide to Compliance for Personal Injury Firms Working With Claims Management Companies' by Paul Bennett

'RTA Allegations of Fraud in a Post-Jackson Era: The Handbook – 2nd Edition' by Andrew Mckie

'RTA Personal Injury Claims: A Practical Guide Post-Jackson' by Andrew Mckie

'On Experts: CPR35 for Lawyers and Experts' by David Boyle

'An Introduction to Personal Injury Law' by David Boyle

'A Practical Guide to Subtle Brain Injury Claims' by Pankaj Madan

These books and more are available to order online direct from the publisher at www.lawbriefpublishing.com, where you can also read free sample chapters. For any queries, contact us on 0844 587 2383 or mail@lawbriefpublishing.com.

Our books are also usually in stock at www.amazon.co.uk with free next day delivery for Prime members, and at good legal bookshops such as Wildy & Sons.

We are regularly launching new books in our series of practical day-to-day practitioners' guides. Visit our website and join our free newsletter to be kept informed and to receive special offers, free chapters, etc.

You can also follow us on Twitter at www.twitter.com/lawbriefpub.

www.ingramcontent.com/pod-product-compliance
Lightning Source LLC
LaVergne TN
LVHW022108200926
848481LV00003B/1112

* 9 7 8 1 9 1 3 7 1 5 8 5 4 *